First Edition

Smart English:

Discussion Questions & Activities
– China

Student Book: Part 2

Intermediate

Andy Smart

Smart English: TEFL Discussion Questions and Activities – China Student Book Part 2

ISBN 978-0-9926912-2-6

First Edition published by Andy Smart 2015

About the Author

England

Born in the UK, Andy Smart has been a qualified teacher since obtaining his PGCE at the University of Brighton in 1990 and has been involved in education ever since. In England he taught at secondary school level for many years and was also strongly connected to work with SEN students including those with severe learning difficulties. This focused on integrating them into mainstream classroom activities in order to achieve their GCSE's and 'A' levels. Later, this commitment led to the establishment of a new day centre and an accompanying curriculum for people with autism. Moving to management in further education, his primary role was in finding placements to meet SEN students' individual requirements as well as setting up and running various outreach projects.

From there Andy's involvement shifted to supporting EBD students who had been excluded from school. His work aimed at guiding young people back onto a pathway, safe from the negative influences of modern society. During this period, his team successfully created a specialised centre for their students' education, fostering the skills needed to survive in the outside world.

Asia

In 2005 Andy relocated to China where he began teaching English to adults in the city of Guilin, Guanxi Autonomous Region. From there he moved to South Korea working in Seoul, teaching young people at academies and also giving private tuition to teenagers in their homes. Returning to China in 2007 he started work in Beijing creating a strong network throughout the city. Since then he has been primarily involved in teaching his spoken English lessons, delivering lectures and training.

In many ways this book is a culmination of years of practice in the classroom. Drawing from a diverse background in education and extensive practice during his time in Asia, Andy has been able to develop a successful learning package aimed at people who want to improve their oral English skills. This is a strong and effective system that promotes fluency, confidence and accuracy, building a platform where the learner comes away with a high level of self achievement. Students therefore start to perceive English in a different manner, instead regarding it as a natural part of their daily life rather than a separate entity that is an ongoing struggle

Contents

22. Science

23. The Supernatural

Appendixes

Appendix A. Grammar at a Glance

Appendix B. Using Phonetics

Preface

Five Types of Student

As a teacher of spoken English, I never quite know who will come into my classroom. It could be someone who has a low English speaking level and is as quiet as a mouse or someone who is both fluent and confident but realises that they are speaking too formally.

One time I was shocked to see one of our most well known IELTS teachers come into the classroom, then sit down with the other students. He had been with our company for many years and his classes were very popular as were his speeches and lectures.

"Why on earth have you come to my class?" I asked feeling puzzled.
"I need to improve my spoken English" he exclaimed.
"You are joking" I laughed. "Really? Your English is great!"
"Yes, but I need to retake my IELTS. My score was too low, so I have to work harder."
"But you're an IELTS teacher. Surely your score was good enough the first time?"
"No, I only got a 7.5 last time" he replied with an unhappy look.
The other students were all astonished at this remark.
"So what score do you need?" I quizzed with great curiosity.
"I need an 8……………..I have to get into Cambridge!"

It just proves that no matter how good you are, you still need to learn to speak more like a native English speaker to really improve. It's a huge advantage in any IELTS or TOEFL exam and is why more and more people are realising that you can't speak proper English if you only learn from a text book. It's one of the big reasons why so many people come to my classes and why these days, learning spoken English is now so popular in China.

Five Types of Student

There are five types of student who can use the Smart English package:

- Students who are doing an IELTS, TOEFL or other English exams. If you are about to do one of these tests then it is essential that you practice your speaking in order to get the score you need. In these lessons you will focus on fluency, pronunciation, grammar and increasing your vocabulary. You will also learn to speak with a higher degree of confidence and freedom from any set models or ideal answers that many text books provide. Remember an examiner can easily spot a candidate reciting. If they do they may choose to ask a follow-up question which will be much harder. It's much better to learn how to answer questions naturally than trying to remember set questions.

- Professionals who need to improve their speaking skills for work. To many professional people, speaking is not just a matter of learning business English. Of course this is an important aspect of communication but in my experience, most just really want to speak to their foreign clients with confidence and accuracy. Many professionals can feel very self-conscious and embarrassed when talking to native English speakers, especially in meetings and on conference calls.

- People who like learning English out of interest. I often get people who come to class purely for their love of the English language. Their main aim is to make English a part of their life becoming 'second nature'. These people have no pressure and no stress and for all, the Smart English package is an extremely agreeable, interesting and fun way to improve.

- People who are going abroad. For anyone who is leaving China to foreign lands, the use of text book English will not be enough to understand what the real native English speakers are saying. Smart English helps the traveller understand informal language and also cultural aspects of where they are going, especially in real life situations such as eating in restaurants or shopping.

- Chinese English teachers who want to move away from a text book model. I have had many IELTS, TOEFL and other traditional English teachers come to class who realise that the formal way Chinese people are taught English in school is only 50% of how to really speak English properly. To these professionals this offers a new dimension and freedom to how their speaking and how they are perceived by both students and colleagues.

Introduction

Learning to Speak Great Spoken English

It's always fantastic when you get positive feedback, so when one of my students came up to me and said

"Andy, why do we love your classes so much?"

I felt fantastic for the rest of the day. You can't beat praise to make you feel good at any time and it's one of the things that you never get tired of hearing. To me the answer to their question is an easy one though. Although these lessons are meant to be fun and interesting they also aim at intensive speaking practice. Actually, students enjoy them so much they don't realise how much speaking in English they are doing. There is less listening to the teacher, less repeating vocabulary and far more emphasis placed on the student doing the work. In fact the teacher should be giving at least 80% student talk time.

Inevitably in any class, the learner will always show some signs of improvement, but here the student will experience a very fast rate of progression. For me, seeing the quietest of students become the most able and outspoken in class always gives me a great feeling of satisfaction. People leave class knowing that they have just spent two hours speaking fluently with pride and confidence and is why they always return to class completing all 66 topics.

The Keys to Speaking Great English

I was speaking to one of our longest serving IELTS teachers the other day. As per usual we ended up comparing the different styles of lesson and how they related to student ability. Whereas my classes focus on the students talking, the IELTS classes are nearly all centered on the teacher doing the work. Indeed the students just listen, watch Power Point and take notes for two hours on exam preparation. I asked him if his hands were tied when it came to the class interacting and practicing speaking.

"Actually, for the Band 6 and 6.5 classes, if I ask my students to speak in English, most will be unable to talk for longer than a minute. After that they will go quiet just sitting there doing nothing. If we try any form of speaking practice, I have to quickly move on and get back to myself doing the talking. The simple problem lies in that they don't learn how to speak English at school. It's not that they don't practice the basics. They drill lexis over and over and learn grammar in the same way. The trouble is that's as far as it goes. They never learn how to develop an argument or conversation in any shape or form".

It always strikes me as odd when a student's note making ability which may be impeccable, in no way matches their ability to verbalise what they have just written. The education system in the PRC instead focuses on reading and writing facilitated by tests and more tests. A student may have a good command of grammar and an extensive vocabulary especially if they are doing IELTS or TOEFL which demand that what you learn is often well outside of what a native speaker uses in daily life. Most students will have already done extensive ground before coming to a spoken English class.

With all the ground work already done, these classes are very different from those you would normally expect to do in 'traditional' lessons. The teacher's job here is merely to create a pathway to encourage putting what the learner already knows into practice.

For me, after a lifetime of acquiring so much unused knowledge, I can only imagine its like learning to drive for years and years but never buying a car. To most students, the key to speaking fluent English is something that is tantalisingly just out of reach.

Confidence

It can't be restated enough that confidence is the single most important thing that you should be getting from any lesson, anytime, anywhere. Confidence confidence confidence is what it's what it's all about! The most confident and relaxed students will always do better in their IELTS or TOEFL exams. Professional people who are confident and relaxed will always be more successful when they are doing business with Western clients.

From confidence comes fluency and from fluency you will become even more confident. It's a wonderful cycle of growth ending in success. When you are achieving fluency and confidence you will become happy in your studies. Going to class will be no longer a chore you have to do. Instead it will become something you want to do. With no stress and pressure, it will become far easier to identify problems and easier to correct them. You will become more accurate in the way you speak and the puzzle will come together as one whole picture.

There are many ways in which you can focus specifically on confidence building. Here is a checklist of what you could be doing.

- Always remember that you have been learning English for a very long time at school. Remember that you already have a large vocabulary in your memory after years and years of repeating vocabulary, doing homework and tests. I am often envious of my students as my Chinese speaking is nowhere near as good as their English. I have to remind myself that whereas I have only been learning for a few years, my students have been learning since they were young.

- Never worry that your English is not as good as your classmate's and that you may look stupid if you don't answer correctly. It's much better to speak than sit quietly, smiling and saying nothing. Remember that if you aren't speaking you aren't practicing.

- Talk talk talk! Try and speak in English as much as possible. Of course speak in Chinese if you really can't understand something and you want to ask a friend. Just remember that you already have a large English vocabulary so take a moment and try and think of an alternative way of saying what you want.

- Talk talk talk! Try and keep away from using your dictionary as much as possible. Just as before, if you can think of an alternative way of saying something then that's much better than stopping your conversation and spending minutes looking in your dictionary. Learn to talk without pausing as this will make you feel really confident.

- When it is breaktime, continue talking in English so it feels like it is a natural thing to do. Watch lower ability students talk in Chinese during breaktime. Remember you can talk in Chinese all you like when class is finished.

- Always ask questions if you don't know. If you are confused about something don't sit there quietly. There will be other students who are also unclear about the same thing. If you understand what you should be doing then you will feel very confident. If you don't understand what you should be doing this is very bad for your confidence. Make sure you know what you should be doing.

- Get into the habit of speaking in English with the class when the teacher is asking questions. When you answer correctly or contribute to the class in English then it will really boost your confidence.

- Try and answer the teacher's questions before your classmates. Don't sit there quietly and wait for someone else to answer. The more you talk, the more the higher ability students will notice you and want to sit with you to practice their English. Knowing this is great for your confidence.

- Make sure you listen to any advice your teacher gives you. Go home and work on it. These classes emphasise that you only need one or two things to work on at a time, so it shouldn't give you too much pressure and shouldn't be too difficult. If you find that suddenly you are improving because you are listening to your teacher, you will become more confident. If you start to make an improvement your teacher will notice and tell you. This is also a huge confidence builder.

- Help your classmates, especially those who are at a lower ability and may be quieter than you. Help them if they don't understand discussions or activities. Help them with pronunciation, grammar and vocabulary. It will make you feel more confident.

- Learn to communicate with your teacher as much as possible. Sit at the front of the class so that your teacher can listen to you as often as possible. This will make you more confident.

1 Common Student Errors

I frequently get worried looking students coming up to me asking me how they can improve their English before their exam. Many are taking it for the second or third time having not attained the score they need to go overseas. Actually most problems are very common, straightforward and identifiable almost immediately. The real issue is that their errors are habitual, having been ingrained since middle school and thus making them really difficult to iron out.

Recently one of my students was scratching her head wondering what she did wrong in her IELTS; after three attempts the highest she'd got was a 5.5 when she really needed at least a 6. She'd been working really hard and clearly things had gotten the better of her. Blowing he nose into a tissue I asked if she was ok

"I catch cold" was her painful reply!

Here is a list of some of the most common mistakes made in class.
- Basic pronunciation errors.
- Some can be referred as 'Chinglish' which means the direct translation from Chinese into English.
- Some things are straight out of a textbook and may have little to do with the real world.
- General poor use of simple grammar. You don't have to be a grammar wiz when it comes to student correction. After a while you will notice that you are correcting the same errors again and again.

Before you start these classes have a look these different problems that many students have when they are speaking in English and see if you recognise any that you may have yourself. Be honest; you want to improve so really think about which ones belong to you. With a pencil, label those that you think you need to practice. Make sure you work on these when you are in class and at home. Show them to your classmates and ask them to let you know when you are making the mistake. During class your teacher may also refer to this list. When they do make a note at the side of the page and make sure you start to correct your errors. You only need to choose one or two from the list and it's very important that you do this work.

Pronunciation

Refer to Appendix B: Using Phonetics. Phonetics are in British English.

Love/Blood/Mud – Phonetics: /ləv/bləd/məd/
Error: /læv/blæd/mæd/
The /ə/ sound is replaced with a pronounced /æ/ saying 'LAV' or 'BLAD'.

Round/Brown/Frown – Phonetics: /raʊnd/ braʊn/fraʊn/
Error: /rɑnd/brɑn/frɑn/
The /aʊ/ is replaced by /ɑ/ sounding like 'RAAND' or "BRAAN'.

Will/Mill/Skill – Phonetics: / wɪl / mɪl / skɪl /
Error: / wiːl / miːl / skiːl /
The /ɪ/ is replaced by / iː / changing the meaning of the word to 'WHEAL, MEAL'.

Usual/Casual/Genre – Phonetics: / juːʒəwəl/ kæʒwəl/ ʒɑnrə
Many students will be able to make the /ʒ/ sound when you ask them, but in normal conversation they will forget it instantly.
Error: /juːjuːɔr/ kæjuːɔr/jɑnrə/
The individual may say 'U YOU AL/, CA YOU AL or YANRE'
Many also have difficulty making the last 'L' sound, instead substituting it with an 'AW' sound, for example, 'U YOU AW' and 'CA YOU AW'.

This/That/Other – Phonetics: / ðɪs / ðæt / əðər
Error: /zɪs / zæt / əzər/
The /ð/ is replaced by /z/ creating 'ZIS, ZAT' or 'OZZER'

Thanks/Author/Mouth – Phonetics: / θæŋks / ɔːθə / maʊθ/
Error: / sæŋks / ɔːsə / pɑːs /
The /θ/ is replaced by /s/ forming 'SANKS', 'AUSOR' or 'MOUSE'

<u>V</u>iolin/<u>V</u>ery/Ha<u>v</u>e – Phonetics: / <u>v</u>aɪəlɪn / <u>v</u>eri ː / hæ<u>v</u> /

Error: /<u>w</u>aɪəlɪn / <u>w</u>eri ː / hæ<u>w</u> /

The /**v**/ is replaced by /**w**/ forming 'WIOLIN', 'WERY' or 'HOW'

<u>Qu</u>ality/<u>Qu</u>antity/<u>Qu</u>alify – Phonetics: /<u>kw</u>ɒləti ː / <u>kw</u>ɒntəti ː / <u>kw</u>ɒləfaɪ /

Error: /<u>k</u>ɒləti ː / <u>k</u>ɒntəti ː / <u>k</u>ɒləfaɪ/ Note the /**w**/ is omitted forming 'KAALITY'.
Also there is not normally any difficulty with 'qui' words such as 'quick' and 'quiet'.

T<u>r</u>agedy/T<u>r</u>ick/T<u>r</u>ee – Phonetics: / træd ʒədi / trɪk / tri ː /

Error: / twædʒədi / twɪk / twi ː /

The /**r**/ is replaced by /**w**/ thus forming 'TWAGEDY' or 'TWICK'.

Towel/Vehicle/ Critical – Phonetics: / taʊəl / vi ː ɪkəl / krɪtɪkəl /

Error: / taʊ ɔ ː / vi ː ɪkɔ ː /krɪtɪk ɔ ː / Here the learner is unable to make the
/**l**/ sound ending the word, instead replacing it with / ɔ ː / forming 'TOWAW' or
'VEHICAW'.

Little/Bottle/Title – Phonetics: / lɪtəl / bɒtəl / taɪtəl /

This is an interesting pronunciation error. In the US, if there is a double or single 't' after
a vowel it is often changed to a 'd' sound. In both British and American English the /**ə**/ is
omitted with the 't/d' and 'l' being made at the same time, for example.

/ lɪtl / bɒtl / taɪtl /

This allows us to focus on making the 'l' clear and pronounced.

Error: / lɪtɔ ː / bɒtɔ ː / taɪtɔ ː /

As above, the /**l**/ is replaced with / ɔ ː / forming 'LITTAW' or 'BOTTAW'. The same
applies to words with a 'd' after a vowel such as 'medal' or 'idle'.

The addition of an unnecessary schwa sound / ə /

Orange/Finish/ Few

Error: / ɒrɪndʒ <u>ə</u> / fɪnɪʃ <u>ə</u> / fju ː <u>ə</u> /

This normally happens after the student has said something that sounds like it ends in a
consonant forming 'ORANGE ER', 'FINISH ER' or 'FEW ER'.

In addition to this, a schwa may be placed in between two consonants, for example,
Adverb/Football/Hardback

Error: / æd ə vɜ ː b / fʊt ə bɔ ː l / hɑ ː d ə bæk /

Sounds like 'ADUVERB', 'FOOTUBALL' or HARDUBACK'.

Chinglish

How do you or can you say (something)?

Error: How to say? / How to spell? This comes from the direct translation of Chinese to English: 'zen me shuo?' / 'zen me pin xie'.

This is the most common mistake made by Chinese students. It is an ingrained habit that you will hear everywhere.

What does it/this mean?

Error: What is meaning? / What's meaning? This comes from the direct translation of 'shenme yisi?' or 'what meaning?'

It's been a while / It's been a long time used if we haven't seen someone for a while.

Error: Although everyone knows '**Long time no see**' we rarely use it. Chinese students may often use this as it is common to say 'Hao jiu bu jian' which is its direct translation.

I like to use the computer/ play computer games

Error: 'I like to play computer' is less of a problem from direct translation, rather than one of laziness that generalises both statements. Firstly it is missing the preposition 'with' and also the possessive pronoun 'my'. Normally we would say 'use my computer' and 'play (computer) games'.

I really like it

Error: 'I very like it'. This unfortunate sentence comes from the translation of 'feichang xihuan' (very like). Unfortunately the Chinese language has no way of modifying a verb as in English which places 'very much' after the verb. In colloquial English we can say 'really like' instead of 'very' before the verb. 'Very enjoy' is another example of this.

Another problem that can occur along side the misuse of 'very' is the confusion between 'like' and 'enjoy'. Because of this you may hear '**I am very liking it**'. The word 'like' expresses a state or condition so it is not used as a continuous verb. If used to give approval of something it can be used in the continuous sense though this is rare.

I have a lot of money

Error: 'I have much money'. This common error originates from the use of 'hen duo' which covers, 'much, many' and 'a lot of'. Most students will be aware that 'a lot of' can be used with both countable and uncountable and that 'many' can be used with countable nouns. However though this is possible, it is not common to use either 'many' or 'much' in positive sentences. Normally we use them with 'do not', for example, 'I don't have much money' or 'There isn't much time to eat dinner'.

Text Book English

Nice to meet you.
Error: This should be used only on the first time of meeting. However, it is often mistakenly used instead of 'Nice to see you (again)'.
'Nice to meet you' is also used formally and may be replaced with something more colloquial.

Q: How are you? A: Fine!
Technically there is no error here but in reality native English speakers rarely ask this question. Though this will vary from country to country we would normally say something far more informal. When we give an answer it is also common to say 'thanks' after our answer followed by 'How about you?'

Basic Grammar

Present v past tense
The most common error you will hear is your students keeping everything in the present tense. Though your students will be aware of its importance, unless you remind them they will naturally keep speaking in the present where it is necessary to be speaking in the past or future. Think of as many activities as you can to keep them focused on it.

Why did you buy this?
Error: 'Why you buy this? / Why you like it?' is missing the auxiliary verb 'do', for example, 'Why did you buy this?' or 'Why do you like it?'

He/She
Because 'ta' is used in Chinese for both male and female (him/her and 'ta de' meaning his or hers), they are frequently misused, for example, 'he is going to have a baby soon' or 'she is going to get married to Susan.'
To Western ears it may sound laughable, but it is a big problem for some learners and another difficult habit to iron out.

Give him/her
Error: 'give he/she'. Here the objective 'him/her' is mistakenly replaced by the pronoun 'he/she'. The object 'him/her' is meant to work with a verb, in this case 'give'.

Give them
Error: 'give he or she' / 'give him or her'. In this case 'them' can be used for anyone without reference to sex. Students may be think that 'them' only refers to the plural and so develop this long winded way of saying things, for example, 'When I have a child, I want him or her to be happy'.

Have and Has

Though they are very important when describing possession or when using the perfect tense, 'have' and 'has' are frequently confused. There are only really a few basic rules to this and they are definitely worth remembering.

For Possession
He <u>has</u> a new car/ I <u>have</u> a new car. Error: 'He have a new car'.
'<u>Have</u>': Used with the pronouns 'I' and 'you' and plural nouns.
1: 'I have a class today' or 'You have a student waiting for you'.
2: 'Students have a lot of pressure', 'We have a class' or 'They have a class'
'<u>Has</u>': Used with the third person singular: 'he, she, it'.
'She has a new student to teach', 'It has a written exam'.

'Have got' and 'has got' have the same meaning, for example, 'I have got no class today' means the same as 'I have no class today'. 'He has got a new student to teach' is the same as 'He has a new student to teach'.

Verb Tenses
Present Perfect
'<u>Have</u>': 'I have been to class a few times', 'You have to read that book one day'.
'<u>Has</u>':   'He had to go to class a few times' or 'It has to be sometime in the near future'.
Past Perfect
'<u>Have</u>': I had to go to class before I start the next semester', 'He had already completed the exam before the class ended' or 'They had gone to the UK before passing their test'.

'Have to' as a modal verb: subject + modal verb (have to/has to/had to) + verb
'I/you/students/we/they have to go to class, 'He/she/it has to get there on Friday',
'I/you/we/they/he/she/it had to'

In four day's time / Four days later

Error: 'In four days <u>later</u>' where past and future become confused. Normally someone is trying to refer to something happening n the past. 'In four days (time)' is a prediction normally attached with 'will be going to' whereas 'later' is a simple way to say afterwards.

Let's go and have dinner/ I want to eat seafood tonight

Error: 'Let's go and have <u>a</u> dinner' or **'I want to eat <u>the</u> seafood tonight'** It is very common for articles 'a, an' and 'the' to be used with uncountable nouns especially when an adjective is preceding it, for example, 'I have a casual clothes'.

You will also hear 'the England' or 'the France'. Most of the time there is no article before a country name unless the name indicates more than one area is covered or it is a republic, for example, The UK, The USA, The PRC, The USSR, The Czech Republic or The Republic of Ireland. Great Britain is excluded from this list though we can say The British Isles.

This is exciting/ I am excited

Error: 'This is excited / I am exciting'. 'Exciting' is an adjective that describes someone's emotion <u>about</u> something. 'Excited' is an adjective <u>informing</u> you that something has influenced your emotions. Other examples that are commonly used are 'boring/bored', 'surprising/surprised' or 'interesting/interested'.

Further problems occur when a present participle (+ing) or past participle (+ 'ed') are used incorrectly. Always use present participles when the noun you are referring to <u>creates</u> the action. If the noun receives the action, use past participles, for example, "The class is interesting" and 'I was interested'.
One single problem that frequently occurs is between the uncountable noun 'health' and adjective 'healthy'.
Error: 'That is bad for your healthy' or 'He is very health'.

There is not enough time

Error: 'There is <u>no</u> enough time' is another common error. 'No' is never used before 'any, much, many' or 'enough'. It can be used in before other adjectives that accompany a noun, for example, 'no fast cars'.

He doesn't have enough time

Error: 'He don't have enough time' should be 'doesn't'.
'I, you, we' and 'they' go with 'don't'.
'He, she' and 'it' goes with 'doesn't'.

Do you have a hobby?

Error: 'Do you have some hobby?' Mistakes involving plurals and singulars are very common. Here it should be either, 'a hobby' or 'some hobbies'. Often the learner is thinking separately and making an incorrect connection between the adjective and noun rather than seeing them together as a single form. Other common errors are: 'There is some', 'There have some', 'The advantages is', 'The book are' and so on.

I need to go shopping

Error: 'I need to go <u>to</u> shopping'. You can't put a preposition before a gerund. This is a mistake where the learner is trying to do too much and is a sign of uncertainty. Can say 'I need to go to the shops' (prep + definite article + noun)

She work<u>s</u> very hard

Error: 'She work very hard'. The simple present tense is one of the most common. Regarding the third person (he, she, it) you must add an 's'. Other errors could be 'He go to work', 'He cook for me' or 'She go by bus'.

I'm mak<u>ing</u> a plan

Error: 'I'm make a plan'. Misuse of the present progressive <u>am</u> + <u>base form</u> + <u>ing</u>
Other examples could be 'She is cook (ing) a meal' or 'I am go (ing) to my office.

2 About the Lessons

Here is a list of the main things that you will be doing in class. Sometimes lessons may be slightly different such as the topic 'Giving Directions' which uses maps. Generally though, you will find that things are done the same way every time. This allows you to become comfortable and familiar with this new approach to learning spoken English.

Brainstorm Vocabulary

This is where your teacher will introduce the topic. However, rather than them doing the work, they will first find out how much you already know about it. Actually you will be surprised at the level of your vocabulary. You will probably find that there are some things you know but can't quite recall. When you finally do remember them, they will most likely stay with you forever, especially if you use them in class during your discussions.

Brainstorming means each person in class can say anything that comes into their mind about the topic. It could be a single word or a phrase; it could be something really simple. The first few students to do this will find it easy, but soon some may start finding it harder than they thought. You will start to try and remember vocabulary that you learnt at school but never used.

There is a space at the beginning of each topic to write down any new or useful words that you can use in class. Write these down and if it helps add the meaning in Chinese next to it. Note down any other useful information that goes with it such as pronunciation, placed in context in a sentence or whether it's a noun (countable or uncountable), verb, phrasal verb, adverb or adjective.

Discussion

Find a partner to talk with in most discussions. Sometimes your teacher will put you into threes or small groups. You may have to change partner from time to time.

Selection of discussion questions are based on the following conditions:
- Usefulness for daily life, especially regarding Western culture.
- Usefulness for IELTS and TOEFL practice.
- Keeping a good balance for all students for any ability.
- Making the topic interesting.
- Keeping things fun and enjoyable.
- Special questions for Chinese people.

Going to the shops, asking for directions and answering the phone are examples of the practical nature of the discussions. If you are going abroad or working with native English speakers, knowledge of how we normally do things will move you from academic, text book English to real life.

The 66 topics cover all areas you may be asked in an IELTS or TOEFL exam. Many questions you will find here are also used in these exams giving you a chance to practice and prepare before the test.

Most topics are aimed at everyone within intermediate level. They are simple and straightforward questions that give everyone a chance to create a conversation in English. There is one topic, 'Space and the Planets' which is at upper intermediate level, but other than that everyone should be able to answer and participate in everything if they have patience and confidence in themselves.

You will get to test your general knowledge of each topic and also learn some amazing new things that you had never thought about before. For example, do you know how many moons there are in the solar system? More than ten? More than fifty? More than 100? If you don't know you will have to wait and find out.

There are many activities which are supposed to be as fun as they are interesting. There is a topic called 'Games and Gambling' where some games are played. Apart from that games are replaced by 'Power Activities'. These are meant to be great fun while practicing spoken English especially all the new vocabulary and useful expressions.

After teaching my spoken English classes in China for so many years, these discussions have been carefully chosen to encourage fast learning and fluency. There are many questions that a native English speaker would find strange but work well with Chinese students, for example, 'What is the best age to get married?' To Western people, it's not a very important thing. Chinese students however, will always go into a long discussion about this; the criteria for deciding a marriage partner is a crucial part of Chinese culture. Because it is something so close to heart, students will always try and express themselves. From this comes fluency followed by confidence.

Repeated Questions

Some questions and activities naturally belong in more than one topic, for example buying something can be found in Banks and Money, Shopping, Numbers and Quantities and Clothes. The big advantage of this if you are doing an IELTS or TOEFL exam is that you can make your job of preparation an easier one. If you see something that is in more than one topic then make a note of it.

Past Tense/Future Tense

The single most common error my students make is when they are supposed to be speaking in the past or future tense. Nearly all will speak in the present tense which of course means they are speaking in Chinglish. It is a terrible habit that must be worked on continually until completely corrected.

Most will know which form they should be speaking in but don't do it. If you are not supposed to be using the present tense, a reminder of which one you should be using has been added after each discussion point.

BTQs

Most new students will never have had a conversation in English before, having only learnt to say a few single sentences at school.
'Break Through Questions' are aimed at making discussion times much longer and move you up into a new level of English speaking. In this case you will find that BTQ's will have a list of easy to answer questions to accompany them, for example

BTQ: **Describe the last gift you bought for someone** (past tense)
Who was it for? What occasion was it? When did you buy it? Why did you choose it? Where did you buy it from? Describe the last gift you received from someone. Who gave it to you and when? Did you like it? Why did they give it to you?

If you are given a BTQ to answer you should be talking for at least five minutes with your partner. BTQs mean that you are really having a conversation in English. They are excellent for your confidence.

Underlined Words

Some things will be underlined. This is meant to stress an important word that you may not know, for example

Shopping: Think three things you should do when bargaining over something?
What are your special ways to 'knock down' the price?

This means 'reduce the price' but it's common in Western countries to say 'knock down'. If you are not sure of the meaning of an underlined word then make sure you ask your teacher.

Devil's Advocate (Power Activity)

This is a special exercise that will make you speak faster, more fluently and with more confidence. It is an excellent warm-up before the roleplay.

I refer to it as a 'Power Activity' because students become visibly stronger within minutes of starting. Power Activities are also a refreshing change from normal classroom methods while still focusing on the spoken English and the relevant topic.

The one thing I've learnt over the years is how much my students all love a good argument. After a few years, I added The Devil's Advocate so that my classes could focus completely on this.

The Devil's Advocate means that whatever your partner says you will totally disagree with them. You will be given an argument by your teacher that you must use against your classmate. You may not personally agree with what your teacher has given you but you must be clever and make an argument based on what you know rather than what you believe, for example

'I hate football!'(soccer)
If I was given this then my partner's argument would be 'I love football'.
I am from England and I am crazy about football. Even so, I would have to disagree with my friend saying that 'It is boring compared to American games. They only kick a ball around and don't score many goals (points). Football players are paid too much when there are poor people everywhere.'

It's incredible what an argument does to unlock someone's speaking potential. The gains from engaging in argument are:
- Less time in translation between Chinese and English. You will focus on what you want to say rather than how to say it.
- You won't be using your dictionary. This means that interaction becomes faster and fluent. Although dictionaries are very useful, they can also slow down a conversation. In this case, if then you can't remember how to say something then you will have to think of other ways to get around the problem.
- You have to use your listening skills in order to make a swift response.
- You will learn to break free from model text book English.
- You will really enjoy yourself.
- If you are nervous, you won't be after five minutes of doing this activity.
- From fluency comes confidence and a great feeling of self achievement. You will feel this strongly at the end of the lesson.

Roleplay

Roleplay is where you practice doing something in real life using English such as going to the shops, answering the phone, borrowing something or asking for advice. My students all love roleplay and are happy to do whatever you give them to play in any scenario without inhibition. Most become very focused on what they are doing and really enjoy speaking in English. Roleplay is an excellent way of learning in that:

- Skills that can be used in real life can be practiced.
- You can get valuable look into Western culture.
- You will further the practice of skills and knowledge learnt during class.
- You will feel no pressure especially if you are about to take your IELTS or TOEFL exams.
- It encourages free speaking away from any set models found in text books.
- You will enjoy and have fun with speaking English.
- Great steps can be made regarding fluency and therefore confidence.

Roleplay (Power Activity)

As I said before, I don't often use games in my lessons, though you can find some in T26: Games and Gambling. Instead I often create situations which depart from real life situations. These normally involve argument or disagreement of some kind but are meant to be really good fun.

Many roleplays are set into two parts. The first is normally based on a normal every day activity such as buying or borrowing something. The second involves argument such as returning the bought item as it is faulty and asking for a refund. In this example the customers complain about the terrible food:

Part 1:
Person A: Waiter or waitress. Welcome your customers. Use Sir or Madame and be as polite as possible. Recommend the Chef's Special. Take their order.
Persons B & C: Customers. Order drinks and an entrée.

Part 2:
Persons B, & C: Customers. That food was terrible. Tell the waiter/waitress why. Refuse to pay the bill.
Person A: Waiter or waitress. It's not your fault. Make excuses for the terrible food. They must pay the bill.

Additional Questions and Activities

Your teacher may want to use material from this section. This is in case the class finishes early, you are doing a 1:1 class or they wish to replace a question or activity that has been previously been done in another topic. You may also use these to practice with a friend when you are not in class.

Vocabulary and Useful Expressions

Normally vocabulary is found at the beginning of the topic. However, in this case it is the last thing found after the additional questions. A Chinese translation is given so you can double check your notes and make sure you leave the classroom understanding everything 100%. There may also be something that you missed in class. Do not read this before the class like you would normally do. If you want to improve and also enjoy the class, read these notes after the class has finished.

3 During Class

If you really want to improve there are many things you can do to quickly raise your ability and level of success. Many students think that all they need to do is come to class and do what the teacher says and that is enough. That's ok but there are many things you can be doing yourself which will significantly improve your spoken English without any effort at all. All you have to do is change some of your habits and ways that you normally do things. Remember that when you are learning to speak fluent English you are also changing yourself as a person.

Before Class

- Set your schedule so that you arrive in class at least ten to fifteen minutes before it starts. There are many reasons for this which will be explained below. Don't arrive exactly on time and of course never late.

- Make sure you have worked on any suggestions your teacher made the lesson before. This may be something they pointed out in the 'common student errors' section. You may not be successful in correcting your problems immediately, but the more you work on them the better you will get. Some things you need to be patient with. Remember that if you have done what your teacher has suggested, they will notice during the next class. Teachers love it if a student has seriously listened to them. It demonstrates that they really want to improve.

- <u>Do not read the next topic before the lesson starts</u>, especially the vocabulary at the end of each topic. This may seem very unusual to you as a Chinese person. In my experience, the most difficult people that come to my classes are Chinese teachers who have learnt how to teach in the 'traditional' way. This is normally reviewing and learning all the vocabulary the night before the lesson so that it is easy to place in context and use in basic sentence structures.

However, the Smart English programme is actually just what it says 'Smart English' because most Chinese people already know a huge amount of vocabulary. During class the teacher will be asking many questions about the topic. You will be surprised at how much you already know and how confident that makes you feel, especially if you have not looked at the vocabulary before hand.

If you answer a question and the teacher says 'well done' then this is a great feeling. You won't get this if you have read the vocabulary before the class; actually you will have the opposite effect.

Eliciting: During class your teacher will elicit as much as possible. Eliciting means that you will be giving the teacher information rather than them doing all the work. There are some great benefits to be made from eliciting if you are a student:

- It is an excellent way for you to use the knowledge that you already have. If you do this it makes you far more confident.
- It makes you much more interested in the topic or discussion point.
- It makes you think about the topic on a deeper level than if the teacher does all the talking.

If there is something you don't know or something you will find useful in the future, make a note of it in the space provided at the beginning of the topic. Writing and analysing new vocabulary in class with your classmates and teacher is a much better way than merely reading the notes at the end of the topic. This way means that information will stay in your brain and is much more effective than reading something.

If you have learnt the vocabulary before the class has started then you will not benefit from this most important aspect of the Smart English programme.

During Class

- Arrive at class ten to fifteen minutes early. This will mean that you will be able to sit with a classmate that you know has the same ability level as you. If you are sat next to someone who is at a higher English speaking level then it may make you less confident, especially if they become frustrated.
- If you are early then you will also be able to sit at the front of the classroom. This is a great benefit if you are interested in improving. It means that you will get to speak with your teacher more often and also they will naturally hear you speaking more than the other students. They will therefore become more familiar with the way you speak and anything you may need to change in order to improve.

By the way, people who sit at the back of the classroom often slip into their bad habits; using their phone or talking too much in Chinese. These are the slow learners.

- Keep off your phone. One of the worst habits my students have is to answer their phone or send messages therefore stopping the activity. If your teacher is explaining something and you are concentrating on your phone, you will not be listening to what you should be doing. In Western countries it is seen as rude if you spend too long on your phone, especially if you leave the room to answer a call. Only do this if it is very important and tell your teacher this before you go.

- Use your dictionary only if you have to. If there is something you don't know then try and think of another way to say it. Remember, you already have a huge vocabulary that you learnt at school so use it. If you still can't think of anything then ask your friend in Chinese to help you. If neither of you can do it only then use your dictionary. You are after all trying to be as fluent as possible. If you are looking at your dictionary then you have stopped talking. The most successful fluent speakers are clever people who can think of alternative ways of saying something.

- Try not speaking Chinese in class. This includes all the small things that we say such as 'thank you, please, correct, sorry/pardon' and 'what does it mean?' Get into the habit of speaking English. The more you do this the better you will get. At breaktime continue speaking in English.

- Make sure you know what these mean before you start these lessons as they are so helpful: *noun, countable and uncountable noun, verb, adverb, phrasal verb and adjective*. You might laugh and say of "of course I know these" but it is surprising how many of my students come to class who don't! Learn these basics and use them often when you are checking on something's meaning.

- Make friends with as many people in class as possible. Get used to changing partners as this will make you become more spontaneous when you are talking. The more friends you have then the more help you will get if you have any problems. Make sure you help others as often as you can.

- When you are talking in English with a classmate, listen to them rather than plan what you are going to say. Listening skills are just as important in any conversation. You need to get into the habit of listening and responding instead of planning. Think about it, do you plan what you are going to say when you are normally speaking in Chinese?

- Listen to your friend and help correct any important errors they make. Some exercises in this book are meant for doing this. Don't worry about upsetting them. You are in class after all and everyone needs to be aware of the things they are not doing correctly otherwise how can you improve?

- Ask questions if you don't understand something. Many students will sit there saying nothing when they don't understand something and then ask their classmate as soon as the activity starts. If are in the habit of doing this then you will start to lose confidence in two ways. Firstly, your classmate will want to start the activity not spend time explaining something again. It's ok to do this for one or two times, but if you continually ask your classmate how to do something they will start to become frustrated. Secondly, it also will promote the feeling that you are not as good as your classmates. This will mean you will be losing confidence.

If you ask your teacher questions because you aren't sure what to do, this will mean that you start the activity with confidence. There will also be people in class who also won't understand and will be relieved that someone has asked.

- When the teacher asks questions, really try and answer them. Don't sit there quietly waiting for the next activity to start. Get into the habit of answering and see how confident you feel.

- Occasionally you will be asked to take turns doing an activity such as in the topic 'Describing Objects'. If so, then volunteer to go first. If you go first then you complete the activity and can then enjoy watching your classmates doing it. This is great for your confidence, especially with no worry or pressure anymore.

- Take notes on new vocabulary or useful expressions. Don't spend too long writing, just the important key points you can use again. You can then quickly refer to them during the activity or after class. Remember that you only get one chance to take notes. You will easily forget them if you don't. I am always surprised when some students don't take notes. People think because it's an English speaking class they need not do this. If you don't then you will miss out on valuable new vocabulary

After Class

- Most students will have only a few really urgent things they need to improve on in their spoken English. Make sure you work on any suggestions your teacher has made. Make this the single most important thing you can do. Your teacher will have identified only one or two things you need to change in order to improve. If you work on this then you can continue to use it in the next class and so on. If you do this, your teacher will notice it and point it out and give you praise. This is a huge confidence builder.

- Do not read the next topic in advance, especially the vocabulary and useful expressions. We have already highlighted why this is so important. Remember you are using the Smart English method not the 'traditional' approach you practiced at school. Trust in the ability that you already have and that you will very soon be speaking fluent spoken English, impressing your colleagues, friends and family.

- Review the most useful and important things from that class as soon as possible. Don't leave doing this until the last minute. Don't make reviewing your notes a chore. Do it as soon as you can and tell yourself that you enjoy doing it. Maybe you can review your notes while you are eating or drinking tea, on the bus or the subway. You only have to read your notes once and hopefully there won't be too many anyway.

4 Topics 1-23

Topic 01

Drink & Drugs

This topic is split into two 1 hour lessons.

Brainstorm Vocabulary

What do you know?

At the beginning of class, think of any vocabulary that you already know along with your classmates. If there is anything you don't know then <u>write it in the space below</u> and practice using it during class. Make sure you understand if it is a noun, verb, adjective or adverb. Make sure your pronunciation is accurate and that you know how to use it in a sentence. Is it formal or informal?

Write new vocabulary and expressions here:

Drugs:
Discussion

1: Think of two illegal drugs
What are they called?
What do they look like?
How do people take them?
What effect does it have after you have taken them?

2: Why do people become addicted to drugs?

3: What punishment should someone who takes drugs receive?
Should the punishment be the same for all drugs?
What punishment should someone get for selling drugs? For which drugs?

4: Once an addict always an addict
Is this true? Is there hope for an addict? Can addicted people be helped?

5: What legal drugs are there?
Are they addictive? Are they bad for your health? Why shouldn't these be made illegal?

Drinking:
Discussion

6: BTQ: Have you ever drunk alcohol before? If not, why not?
Work in groups of three. If anyone hasn't drunk any alcohol before then listen to your classmates and ask them questions.
If you did, did you enjoy it? Where, when, who with and what happened?
Have you been drunk before? Tell your story. (past tense)

7: What punishment should a drunk driver receive? Why?
What would you do if your friend was drunk and wanted to drive home?
What would you do if they had just one or two drinks?

Devil's Advocate

You should not be allowed to drink and get drunk in the street.

Role Play

Drunk Driving
Person A: Police officer. You have caught this person drunk driving. You hate people who do this. Take them down to the police station immediately.
Person B: Drunk driver. Make some big excuses and try and avoid punishment.

Gate-crasher
Work in small groups.
Person A and B: Gatecrashers. You have no ticket or invitation to get into the party. Try and persuade the doorman to let you in. Be persistent. Make up a story.
Person C: Doorman. Refuse to let anyone in with no initiation or ticket. You are not allowed to accept money.

Finish Class

Additional Questions and Activities

1: Teacher's Handy Party Tips
These can be found in Book 01, Topic 10: Parties.
These are designed as life savers for anyone who has not been on a typical Western night out. Follow these tips for an enjoyable night or ignore them at your peril.

2: Why do people smoke?
A: Surely it is totally crazy! Do you think smoking is a good or bad thing? How does it affect your health? Would you marry a smoker?

B: What advice could you give someone who wanted to stop smoking?

C: Which of the following would be the best way to reduce smoking? What would the advantages or advantages in each case?

- Treble the price of cigarettes.
- Make smoking illegal.
- Launch a public health campaign.
- Limit smoking to very specific areas.
- Something else.

3: Does drinking change your personality?
How do people that have had a few drinks behave?
What happens to you when you drink?

Devil's Advocate

Alcohol companies should not be allowed to advertise.

If alcohol can be advertised then cigarettes should be allowed too.

I love going to clubs and bars.

There should be strict laws for which age someone can be allowed to start drinking alcohol and smoking cigarettes.

Role Play:

Alcoholic Employee
Person A: Boss. Your employee is always coming to work smelling of alcohol. You found a bottle of baijiu in their desk. Tell them that their drinking must stop immediately.
Person B: You are under a lot of pressure at work and at home. Explain to the boss.

Cigarette Company

Part 1: (optional)
Person A: Government representative. Announce that from now on cigarette companies will be allowed to advertise in China.
Person B: CCTV interviewer. Continually ask follow up questions? Why is this being allowed? Where will they be allowed to advertise? Won't this affect people's health?

Part 2:
Each group owns a cigarette company. They have made a new brand of cigarettes.
Think of the target consumers who will buy the product.
Think of the name of your cigarettes.

Part 3:
Group A: Your company has a new brand of cigarettes. Give them to people to sample outside a supermarket.
Group B: Customers. You hate cigarettes and what they do to people. Strongly voice your disapproval to these people. Be angry.

Weight loss pills
Can be in pairs or small groups.

Person A: Your company has some new weight loss pills. They work very well.
Sell them to some customers in a supermarket.
When should they be taken? How many? How much weight will they lose?
Person B: Customers. You do think you are overweight. Ask the salesperson about these tablets.
Do they have any side effects? How are they tested? Do they really work?

Vocabulary and useful expressions

Drugs
Street names (informal name for drugs)
Grade A: hard drugs：<口>（会在生理和心理上）致瘾的麻醉品, 毒品
Addictive：上瘾的, illegal：违法的
Heroin/smack：海洛因, inject：注射, crack/rocks：一种高纯度可卡因毒品,
Cocaine/coke/Charlie：可卡因 snort：吸食(毒品)
Ecstasy/ E /pills：迷幻药
Grade C: soft drugs：软性毒品, non-addictive：（毒品等）不致瘾的
Marijuana/cannabis/weed：大麻, solids：固体, roll a joint：模拟卷烟
Legal: tobacco：烟草, nicotine：尼古丁, prescription drugs：处方药,
anti-depressants: 抗抑郁药, Prozac：百忧解（一种抗抑郁药）

Drinking
White wine：白葡萄酒, red wine：红葡萄酒, sweet and dry：甜的或无甜味的葡萄酒,
champagne：香槟
Beer：啤酒, lager：窖藏啤酒
Cider：苹果酒
Spirits：烈酒, neat：未掺水的酒
Soft drinks：不含酒精的饮料
Cocktails：鸡尾酒, punch：一种混合了果汁和酒的饮料
Alcoholic：含酒精的, rehab' (rehabilitation)：修复、康复
Teetotal：完全戒酒的

Topic
02 Hospitals

Brainstorm Vocabulary

What do you know?

At the beginning of class, think of any vocabulary that you already know along with your classmates. If there is anything you don't know then <u>write it in the space below</u> and practice using it during class. Make sure you understand if it's a noun, verb, adjective or adverb. Make sure your pronunciation is accurate and that you know how to use it in a sentence. Is it formal or informal?

Write new vocabulary and expressions here:

Discussion

1: Think of four reasons to go to hospital.
You are not allowed to say for a cold, the flu, as your job or to visit relatives who are sick.

2: Would you <u>make</u> a good surgeon? Why or why not?
Would you like to be one? What qualities does a good surgeon need to have?

3: Would you give blood?
Would you donate your organs after you die? Why or why not?

4: Is it ok to pay extra to get better treatment?
Have you or a relative ever paid to get faster treatment? What is your opinion about this?
How much extra did you or they have to pay? Was it worth it?

5: Operating Procedure
If you were a surgeon performing (doing) an operation what should you do?
Work through this with your teacher.
Write the answers in sequence below:
1: What is the first thing you should do?
2: What's next?
3: What do you use to do the operation?
4: First part of the operation:
5:
6:
7:
8: How do you finish the operation?

6: What is your opinion of people who have cosmetic surgery?
What is the difference between plastic surgery and cosmetic surgery?

Think of five different types of cosmetic surgery, for example, in South Korea it is really popular for people to have their eyes changed.

Think of a famous person who has had bad cosmetic surgery. Do they look better than before?

7: CPR
If you saw someone lying <u>unconscious</u> lying at the side of the road what would you do and why? What should you do?

If someone <u>passed out</u> now in this classroom what would you do?

Role Play

Perform an operation
You can print off the role play, including flash cards though these aren't necessary.
If you use the flash cards allow them a few minutes to use their dictionaries.
Put the students into small groups or pairs.

Person A: Surgeon. You have to do a small operation on someone. Tell the relatives what you need to do. Tell them your plans for the operation.
Person B & C: Relatives. You are very worried about this. Continually ask questions. How long will it take? Is it dangerous? Will they need anesthetic? Can they eat and drink before and after? When can they return to normal life?

Finish Class

Additional Questions and Activities

1: What are the first five words you think of when you hear the word 'hospitals'?
Write them down as fast as you can.

2: What problems are there with the health care system in China?
What solutions can you think of?

3: What do people do if they can't afford to go to hospital?

4: What health problems do older people have?
How can we help them?

5: BTQ: **Talk about the last time you had to go to hospital.** (past tense)
Only talk about something you feel comfortable about for example, for a broken bone or X-ray etc.
How do you feel in hospitals?
When did you go? What was this hospital like? Clean, noisy or crowded?
How long were you there?

6: How does stress affect your health?
What illnesses can be caused by stress? How does stress affect your body?

Devil's Advocate

There are limited beds in hospitals. We should not give them to people who have smoking related illnesses.

Employees should be sent on basic CPR training for their company.

Role Play:

Job Interview
You can use the interview questions found in T14.

Person A: You are the director of a hospital. You need to hire a new doctor. Interview a specialist for the job. Ask interview questions. Ask follow up questions.

Person B: Specialist. What is your specialism? Answer all the questions. You cannot say "I don't know". Talk about your successful operations.

A Check up
Person A: Son/Daughter. You are worried about your Mum/Dad's health these days. They are getting old now. Persuade them to go to the hospital for a check up.

Person B: Parent. Be stubborn. You rely on traditional Chinese medicine for any health problems. You don't want to go to the hospital.

Vocabulary and useful expressions

Anatomy：解剖
Skeleton：骨骼, bones：骨, skull：头骨, collar bone：锁骨, rib cage：胸腔,
 pelvis：骨盆 Muscles：肌肉, biceps：二头肌, thigh muscle：大腿肌肉
Organs：器官, eyes：眼睛, stomach：胃，腹部, heart：心脏 liver：肝脏,
kidney：肾脏, lungs：肺
Surgeon：外科医生, paramedic：护理人员
A&E (Accident & Emergency): 急诊室
Operation：手术, anesthetic (local/general)：麻醉剂（局麻/全麻），
Scalpel：外科手术刀, sterilize：消毒, Unconscious：无意识的，
CPR：心肺复苏术, pulse：脉搏

Topic
03 Common Health Problems & First Aid

Brainstorm Vocabulary

What do you know?

At the beginning of class, think of any vocabulary that you already know along with your classmates. If there is anything you don't know then <u>write it in the space below</u> and practice using it during class. Make sure you understand if it's a noun, verb, adjective or adverb. Make sure your pronunciation is accurate and that you know how to use it in a sentence. Is it formal or informal?

Write new vocabulary and expressions here:

Discussion

1: Think of three minor health problems we would not go to see a local doctor for.
How would you treat it?

2: If you burnt your hand in the kitchen what should you do?
   If you cut your hand in the kitchen what should you do?

Answer in one or two sentences. Give simple but perfect English.

3: Think of three health problems we would go to the local doctor for.

4: Colds and Flu
What is the difference between a cold and the flu?
What are the <u>symptoms</u> of cold or flu?
How do you catch the flu?
Where are the most likely places to catch the flu and why?

5: BTQ: Describe the last time you got the flu or a cold? (past tense)
When was it and where?
How long did it last?
How did you feel?
Did you stay at work/college? Did you have time off?
Did you take any medicine?

If you can't remember then pick any other minor sickness.

6: Pain
Think of one or two different areas of pain, for example, ear ache.
Your teacher will also give you some examples. They will be very useful.

7: Would you make a good nurse? Why or why not?

8: Traditional medicine
What traditional Chinese medicines or techniques do you know?
Have you used them? What for?
Were they effective?
One example is acupuncture.

9: Think of three questions the doctor may ask their patient.
Write them down.

Role Play

Go to the doctors
Use the sentences you wrote down from Q9.
<u>Person A:</u> You are sick. Go and see the doctor for help.
<u>Person B:</u> Doctor. Ask the patient questions. Give them some advice and try to sell them your most expensive medicine.

Finish Class

Additional Questions and Activities

1: First Aid box
What would you keep in your first aid box at home? Think of five things.

2: How is mental health related to physical health?
If you are feeling stressed, lonely, worried or depressed how can this affect your physical health?

Devil's Advocate

Computers are bad for your health.
You should limit the number of hours you spend using your lap top.

You should not eat in restaurants if possible.
Its best to cook at home where you know the food is safe.

It's ok going to bed late. It does nothing to upset your health.

Role Play

New Medicine
<u>Person A:</u> Your chemist has a new kind of medicine. Everyone should have it at home. It is amazing! Sell this new product to some customers in a shopping mall. What does it do? Is it a liquid or in tablet form? How many times a day should it be taken and when?
<u>Person B:</u> Customers. Continually ask follow up questions. You don't believe it can be so effective. How has it been tested?

Check up at the doctors

Person A: Go for a check up at the doctors. You are a workaholic, working seven days a week under a lot of pressure. You don't eat properly and neglect your family. Recently you have had some bad chest and stomach pains.

Person B: Doctor. This person will have some serious health problems if they are not careful. Recommend immediate changes in lifestyle; exercise, relaxation, better food. What parts of their body are at risk?

Person A: Disagree with the doctor. It is impossible to change.

Doctor's note

In the UK we can get a doctor's note to give to our employer if we are sick. If you have a doctor's note, you may be entitled to sick pay from your company. A doctor's note will have a specific number of days you can be absent.

In the UK if we phone up our company and say we are unable to work because we are ill we call this 'pulling a sickie'. It is normally negative as it implies that you aren't as ill as you are saying or you stayed up too late the night before and are not really ill. In this case 'pulling a sickie' is a form of deception.

Part 1:

Person A: You are sick and you need time off of work. You have a few other important things you need doing this week. Phone your boss and tell them you are really sick. Make it sound that it is much worse than it is.
Person B: Boss. It sounds like they are acting. Ask them some questions about their illness.

Part 2:

Person A: You are sick and you have had time off of work. You already told your boss you need a week off. Go to the doctors and get a five day doctors note. Make it seem like your problem is much worse than it really is.
You must be successful.
Person B: Doctor. Ask the doctor's questions from the white board. You don't think it's that serious. Give them a two day doctor's note.

Hypochondriac

Person A: Patient. You are sure you have many things wrong with you. Go and see the doctor for help. Your health is in big trouble.
Person B: Doctor. Ask the doctor's questions from the white board. You can't find anything wrong at all with this person. They could be wasting your time.

Vocabulary and useful expressions

Influenza, the flu：流行性感冒

Transmitted：传播, airborne：空气传播的, saliva：唾液, sneezing：打喷嚏,

Coughing：咳嗽

A check up：检查

Fever：发烧, dehydrated：脱水的, a temperature：<口>发烧, sweating：发汗,

A chill：发冷

Symptoms：症状, cause：原因, diagnosis：诊断, treatment：治疗, prescribe：给医嘱

Tablets：药片, pills：药丸, capsules：胶囊, anti-biotics：抗生素

Pain: 疼痛 shooting：刺痛, stabbing：刺穿的, throbbing：抽痛, searing：灼热的

Ache: eye：眼睛痛, back：后背痛, head：头痛, ear：耳朵痛

Sore throat：喉咙痛

Agony：极大的痛苦

Migraine：偏头痛

Chemist (UK), pharmacy, drug store (US): 药房

Prescription：处方

Doctor's note：医生的证明, 'pulling a sickie'(UK)：病假

Topic
04 Health & Fitness

Brainstorm Vocabulary

What do you know?

At the beginning of class, think of any vocabulary that you already know along with your classmates. If there is anything you don't know then <u>write it in the space below</u> and practice using it during class. Make sure you understand if it is a noun, verb, adjective or adverb. Make sure your pronunciation is accurate and that you know how to use it in a sentence. Is it formal or informal?

Write new vocabulary and expressions here:

Discussion

1: What are the keys to a healthy and happy life?
Answer Check and record anything useful on the white board.

2: Obesity
These days it is very common to see people who are overweight. Why do so many people become too heavy? How have our lifestyles changed in recent years for this to happen?

3: Think and describe five types of exercise you can do at home.

4: Over exercise
What happens to people who exercise <u>aggressively</u> every day for long periods of time?

5: Body clock

A: How important is it to go to bed at the 'right time' every night? What is the right time? What happens to you if you go to bed too late? How do you feel the next day? How does it affect your daily routine, including what and when you eat? Does it have a <u>knock-on effect?</u>

B: Talk about the last time you went to bed too late (past tense).
When, why, how did you feel the next day? Do you often stay up late?

6: Think of five ways to lose weight.

7: What is a vegetarian? What can a vegetarian eat?
Would you like to be a vegetarian? Why or why not?
What are the advantages and disadvantages of being a vegetarian?
If you only eat fish and not meat are you still a vegetarian?

8: Low income families
Why does having a low income affect a family's health?

Devil's Advocate

There is no need to exercise and be too strict with your diet.
It's ok to be unhealthy at times.

Role Play

Weight loss pills
Work in pairs or small groups.

Person A: Salesperson. Your company has some new weight loss pills. They work very well. Sell them to some customers in a supermarket.
When should they be taken? How many? How much weight will they lose?
Person B: Customers. You do think you are overweight. Ask the salesperson about these tablets. Do they have any side effects? How are they tested? Do they really work? How should I take them?

Finish Class

Additional Questions and Activities

1: Anorexia and Bulimia
Many people also under eat. Some people suffer from anorexia or bulimia.
Why do people suffer from these problems?

2: Why do people smoke?
A: Surely it is totally crazy! Do you think smoking is a good or bad thing? How does it affect your health? Would you marry a smoker?

B: What advice could you give someone who wanted to stop smoking?

C: Which of the following would be the best way to reduce smoking? What would the advantages or advantages in each case?

- Treble the price of cigarettes.
- Make smoking illegal.
- Launch a public health campaign.
- Limit smoking to very specific areas.
- Something else.

3: Personal hygiene
Give five things you have to do to maintain personal hygiene every day.

4: Teeth
How often do you brush your teeth?
How often do you change your toothbrush?
When was the last time you went to the dentist? What for?
How often you go for a check up?
Do you have perfect teeth?
Would you like to be a dentist?

5: Are you 100% healthy?
What are the healthiest and most unhealthy things you do in your life?

Devil's Advocate

It's healthy being a vegetarian.

I can stay on my computer all day and feel ok.

E: Role Play

Special classes for the seriously overweight
Person A: Gym owner. You want to start some classes, three times a week for people who are overweight. Hire a professional to run the classes.
Ask interview questions. What is your experience? How long have you been doing this?
Person B: Professional. Why do you want the job? Why did you become a fitness instructor? What ideas do you have to make these classes successful?

Check up at the doctors

Person A: Go for a check up at the doctors. You are a workaholic, working seven days a week under a lot of pressure. You don't eat properly and neglect your family. Recently you have had some bad chest and stomach pains.
Person B: Doctor. This person will have some serious health problems if they are not careful. Recommend immediate changes in lifestyle; exercise, relaxation, better food. What parts of their busy are at risk?
Person A: Disagree with the doctor. It is impossible to change.

Health Spa

Part 1:
Have you ever been to a health spa before? What was it like and what did you do there? If not would you like to go to one?
Think of five things you can do at a health spa.

Part 2:

<u>Person A:</u> Congratulations. You have won a prize for a weekend at a luxury health spa. Go to the reception desk and <u>check in</u>. Continually ask questions about its facilities.

<u>Person B:</u> Manager. Welcome your guests and introduce them to the health spa. Tell them about their room, the food, the <u>facilities</u> and the and about the treatments and therapies that are available to them for the weekend.

Vocabulary and useful expressions

Pull-ups：引体向上, sit-ups：仰卧起坐, push-ups：俯卧撑, star jumps：跳跃运动, squat thrusts：下蹲后促腿动作

Muscles：肌肉 stretch：伸展, warm-up：准备动作，热身

Obesity：肥胖症, comfort eating：安慰性饮食

Body clock：生物钟, knock-on effect：连锁反应

Hygiene：卫生学，保健法

Facilities：设备

Sauna：桑拿浴, jacuzzi：按摩浴缸, manicure：修指甲, waxing：打蜡（除毛），

Aromatherapy：芳香疗法, meditation：冥想

Topic
05 Sport

Brainstorm Vocabulary
What do you know?

At the beginning of class, think of any vocabulary that you already know along with your classmates. If there is anything you don't know then <u>write it in the space below</u> and practice using it during class. Make sure you understand if it's a noun, verb, adjective or adverb. Make sure your pronunciation is accurate and that you know how to use it in a sentence. Is it formal or informal?

Write new vocabulary and expressions here:

Discussion

1: What is a sport?
Generally we think of competitive sports, though there are 'outdoor sports' and 'extreme sports' where there are no winners or losers.
Are jogging and yoga sports?

2: BTQ: What is your favourite sport?
This appears to be an easy question. However, if you get this in an IELTS or TOEFL exam then you will be expected to answer such an easy question perfectly.

To help you, first write down as many key words as you can for your favourite sport in two minutes.

Next, practice talking for two minutes each with your partner.
You should aim for fluency, no 'ums' and 'ers' and good grammar.

3: Track Events:
Think of and describe two track events, for example, 100metres.
Which would you rather do; the marathon or 100m? Why?

4: Talk about an athlete you admire.
What qualities do they have that make them great?

5: Which is the most boring sport? Why?

6: How do you play badminton?
Use simple verbs and sequencing such as 'First, second, next' and 'finally'.

7: How should an athlete prepare before a match/game?

Devil's Advocate

Team sports are better than sports for individuals.

Role Play

Interrupt your opponent
Work in groups of three if you can.

Person A: You are a CCTV interviewer at the Olympics before the 100m's race.
Interview some of the competitors before the race.
How are they feeling?
How did they prepare?
Are they feeling confident?
Why do they think they will beat their opponent?

Person B & C: Competitors. You don't like each other. You both think that you will win.
You think you are better than the other. You think you are a natural winner.
Continually interrupt your opponent when they are answering questions.

International volley ball team
Your teacher will put you into groups.

Person A: You are the coach of China's national volley ball team. Last game you played
you lost against South Korea. The next game is against Japan at the Birds Nest.
Xi Jinping will be there to watch it. YOU MUST WIN.
Create a training plan for your team. Think about diet, sleeping times, exercises, attitude
and lifestyle. BE <u>STRICT</u>.
Person B, C & D: The team. You think your coach is too strict. You work very hard
already. Continually disagree with your coach.

Finish Class

Additional Questions and Activities

1: What were your favourite sports at school and why? (past tense)
What were your least favourite sports and why?

2: What is the most unusual sport and why?
Describe it.

3: What is the most dangerous sport and why?

4: Why do people cheat in sport?
How do people cheat?
What should happen to people who cheat in sport?

5: Give three reasons why the Chinese football team is so bad.
There are only eleven players in a football team and 1.3 billion people in China.

6: Think of three types of 'blood sport'
What is your opinion of these? Are some ok and some not? Why?

7: Think of three types of 'extreme sport'
Why do people do extreme sports? Is there one you would like to try?

8: Do you prefer team sports or those for individuals? Why?

9: Which form of tennis is best? Doubles or singles? Why?

Devil's Advocate

The Olympics is better than the Football World Cup

If China is to win the World Cup one day, football should be taught in middle school and high school.

I love basketball.

Boxing is a terrible sport that should be banned.

Role Play

Watch the game live or on TV
Person A: You want to go to see some <u>live</u> sport. You don't want to go alone. Persuade your friend to go with you. You have already bought tickets.
Person B: You don't want to go. It's easy to watch it on TV.

Yao Ming school visit
Work in small groups of three or four.
Person A: You are Yao Ming. You are visiting a school in Beijing to open its new sports ground and gymnasium on CCTV. Meet some of the children and answer their questions.
Person B, C & D: Children. You are very excited. Ask Yao Ming some questions.

Vocabulary and useful expressions

Competition：竞赛, tournament, championship：锦标赛
Referee, umpire, judge：裁判员
Athlete：运动员
Football (UK): 足球, soccer (US): <美>足球；
American football (US): 美式橄榄球, rugby：英式橄榄球
Winner：优胜者, runner-up：亚军, loser：失败者, 'wooden spoon'：末名，最后一名
Track events：竞赛项目, hurdles：跨栏赛, baton：接力棒, 100m,
Marathon,：马拉松赛跑 steeplechase：障碍赛跑
Equipment：装备, shuttlecock：羽毛球, net：网, court：网球场

Topic 06

Games & Gambling

A fun and energetic topic with games and discussion together.
All games are aimed at practicing spoken English.

Brainstorm Vocabulary

What do you know?

At the beginning of class, think of any vocabulary that you already know along with your classmates. If there is anything you don't know then <u>write it in the space below</u> and practice using it during class. Make sure you understand if it is a noun, verb, adjective or adverb. Make sure your pronunciation is accurate and that you know how to use it in a sentence. Is it formal or informal?

Write new vocabulary and expressions here:

Discussion

1: What games did you play as a child? (past tense)
Where did you play them? Who with? Were you good at it? Did you win?

2: Do you play the lottery? Why or why not?
If you played, have you ever won anything? What is your opinion of the lottery?

Activity

Word Association

When your classmate says one word what do you <u>associate</u> with it?
For example, if they said 'green' you may reply 'tree, plant, new, sick, red, colour,' and so on. Whatever you say, the classmate on your other side must then think of a word which associates with it. This will then continue quickly around the class.

There are only three rules for this
1. If you repeat what someone else has said then YOU ARE OUT!
2. If you wait/pause for longer than 10 seconds then YOU ARE OUT!
3. No helping classmates.

The last person is the winner.

Activity

Guess the famous person
One student should come to the front of the class and take a card from the bag.
Do not let anyone else see it.
It will have the name of a famous person on it.

The class can ask one simple '**yes/no**' question each, for example, "Are they dead? Are they a woman? Are they a politician?"

Discussion

3: Computer games
What is your opinion of people who play computer games? Have you ever played any computer games? Which ones? How many hours did you play?
Are they a waste of time?

Devil's Advocate

Gambling should be made legal.
Betting is legal all over the world.
You can gamble in Macau and Las Vegas. Why not China?

Activity

Two truths and a lie

Part 1:
Your teacher will write two true sentences and one false one about themselves on the white board. You must ask them questions to try and find out which one is the false one.
Beware: Your teacher may be lying to you!

Part 2:
Work individually.
Take 5 minutes to write down three sentences about yourself. Two should be true and one should be a lie.

Part 3:
Work in groups of three.
Take 5 minutes each to take turns trying to work out which of your classmates' statements is a lie.

Finish Class

Additional Questions and Activities

1: Why do people cheat in sport?
How do people cheat?
What should happen to people who cheat in sport?

2: Why is gambling addictive?

3: When you are a parent, what games would you think would be suitable for your kids to play?
Would you let them play computer games? Why or why not?

4: How have children's games changed since you were at school?

5: How do you play table tennis?
First elicit the equipment used; net, bat, table and ball. Badminton is played on a court. Write these on the white board.
Use simple verbs and sequencing such as 'First, second, next' and 'finally'.

6: TV quiz show
Talk about a popular TV quiz show. Why is it popular and do you like it?
What's your opinion of TV quiz shows?
Would you go on one? Why or why not?

Devil's Advocate

Computer games are a waste of time

Vocabulary and useful expressions

Deck/pack of cards：一副纸牌，
Suit (Hearts, Diamonds, Clubs, Spades): 纸牌中的花色（红桃，方块，梅花，黑桃）
Ace, Jack, Queen, King：纸牌中分别代表 A、J、Q、K
Poker：纸牌

Gambling junkie：赌博上瘾, computer junkie：电脑迷, addicted：上瘾的
Place a bet：下注
Lottery ticket：彩票
Roulette：轮盘赌, slot machine：老虎机, one armed bandit：赌博机

Topic

07 Hobbies & Spare Time Activities

Brainstorm Vocabulary

What do you know?

At the beginning of class, think of any vocabulary that you already know along with your classmates. If there is anything you don't know then write it in the space below and practice using it during class. Make sure you understand if it is a noun, verb, adjective or adverb. Make sure your pronunciation is accurate and that you know how to use it in a sentence. Is it formal or informal?

Write new vocabulary and expressions here:

Discussion

1: What hobbies did you have as a child? (past tense)

2: Are hobbies important? Why or why not?
In some countries like South Korea, studying and work is far more important than pursuing a hobby. In the West some people will have a lot of different interests.

Do we really need hobbies? Maybe we are just wasting our time?
How important are hobbies to you?

3: Your schedule
Talk about your daily schedule with your partner. How much free time do you have every day and when? What do you do with your free time? Do you do anything interesting? How about the weekends? Do you have more time then to pursue your interests?

4: If you could start a new hobby tomorrow what would it be and why?

5: Outdoor Pursuits
In the West lots of people love outdoor pursuits. The sale of outdoor pursuits has been a huge industry for a long time.

Think of and describe five types of outdoor pursuits.

BTQ: When was the last time you went out hiking in the country?
When, where and who did you go with? How did you get there? What did you have to eat? Did you stay there? Did you enjoy it? How was the weather? (past tense)

6: Camping
If you were going camping in the mountains for a fortnight, think of five things you would like to take with you. Why would you take them?
Think of two important survival tips for living in the wilderness.

Role Play

Invite your friend to go hiking
Person A: You love being in nature. You want to go hiking this weekend. You don't want to go alone. Persuade your friend to go with you. Be very persistent.
Person B: You are not interested. You like your sofa, pizza, your computer and restaurants. You don't want to go.

Collecting

Students think of one thing people like to collect. Your teacher will make a list on the white board.

Person A: You are crazy about collecting (*choose one from the list*). You want to start a club. Persuade your great friend to be the first one to be in your club. You really want them to join. Never give up.
Person B: You really have no time for this. It's a pointless hobby. Tell your friend you are not interested.

Change places. Choose another collectable something from the list.

Finish Class

Additional Questions and Activities

1: Think of and describe five hobbies you do at home.

2: Think of and describe five hobbies that don't cost anything.

3: Procrastinating and time wasting
What kind of person are you? Do you always do things straight away or do you put off things until the next day? Give examples.

When do you waste your time?
What do you do when you waste time?
How much time do you waste?
What other more useful things could you be doing instead? Why don't you do them?

4: Describe a hobby that someone in your family may have.
How long have they been doing it? Have you had a try?

5: Is it a good idea to change your hobby into a business?
Why or why not?

6: Extreme Sports
What does 'extreme' mean and why do we use it in sport?
Have you ever tried an extreme sport? Describe your experience.
Would you like to try one? Why or why not? If yes, which one?

Devil's Advocate

It's a good idea to turn your hobby into a business.

Computer games are a waste of time.

I don't like outdoor activities.

E: Role Play

Camping shop
Person A: You want to go camping but have never been before. Go to an outdoor shop and ask for advice. Also what equipment should you buy and how should you use it? Continually ask the shop assistant questions.
Person B: Shop assistant. Answer all the questions.

Turn your hobby into a business.
Person A: You have a great idea to turn your hobby into a business.
Tell your friend and persuade them to go into business with you.
You really want them to join you. Never give up.
Person B: You think it's a terrible idea. Politely think of excuses to say no.

School outdoor activities weekend
Person A: Teacher. You have arranged an outdoor activities weekend for the kids. They are between 8 and 10 years old.
Tell the parents your plans for the weekend.
Key words: *camping, hiking, collecting things, drawing and horse riding.*
Person B: Parent. Of course you are worried about your child going away for the first time. Continually ask the teacher questions.
Key words: *safety, weather, food, transport, where will they stay?*

Household Chores
Person A: Parent. You work late. Often you don't get any time to do the housework.
You have two teenage children (B and C) who hardly do any chores to help around the house. They are extremely lazy.
B: Does some housework but not much. They put the dirty plates in the kitchen but never wash up. Sometimes they tidy their dirty clothes up.
C: Does nothing and is really untidy. They leave food and dirty clothes everywhere. They leave the lights on.
Be angry with them and tell them they must start to do the chores.

Person B: You do some housework but not much. Make it sound like you do more.
　　　　　Continually interrupt your brother/sister.

Person C: You never do anything. Take credit for what your brother/sister does.
　　　　　Say that you did it. Continually interrupt your brother/sister.

Vocabulary and useful expressions

Extreme sports：极限运动, adrenaline: [生化] 肾上腺素, addictive：上瘾的
Outdoor pursuits：户外运动
Tent：帐篷, camping：露营
Equipment：装备
Survival tips：急救技巧, wilderness：荒野

Topic
08 D.I.Y.

Brainstorm Vocabulary

What do you know?

At the beginning of class, think of any vocabulary that you already know along with your classmates. If there is anything you don't know then <u>write it in the space below</u> and practice using it during class. Make sure you understand if it's a noun, verb, adjective or adverb. Make sure your pronunciation is accurate and that you know how to use it in a sentence. Is it formal or informal?

Write new vocabulary and expressions here:

Discussion

1: Have you ever done any repair of your home or home improvements?
What did you do? Why? Were you successful? (past tense)
Have any of your parents or relatives done any work on your home?
What did they do and why? (past tense)

Put your class into three's if you can.

2: Think of three tools you use for home improvement.
What do you use them for? Think of any verbs that you use with them.
Elicit one tool such as a hammer as an example before hand.
Answer Check and put anything useful on the white board.

3: Use the worksheets 'Painting & Decorating' and 'DIY Tools'
   Go to the 'Vocabulary and Additional Questions' section below.

Why do you use a screwdriver for painting? Opening the lid of the can!
What do we use the various tools for?

4: Screw driver, paint, roller and roller tray (2, 3, 5 and 7)
Describe how you use them to paint the wall. Use sequencing such as 'first, second, next and last' with some simple verbs.

5: When you have children what do you want their bedroom to look like?
Include colour, paintings, places for their toys, lights and music.
Be creative.

6: If you could change the look of where you live, how would you change it?
It could be your home apartment or dormitory.
It could be the walls, floors, ceiling, doors, furniture; anything.
Think of three things.
Why would you change it?

Devil's Advocate

We should all learn DIY at school (woodwork/metalwork).

Role Play

Power Tools: Buy an electric drill

Take two or three minutes to read the instructions on the page in the 'Vocabulary and Useful Expressions' section.

Pick out one or two verbs from each sentence including the phrasal verbs.

Worksheet 2: Work in pairs and use the diagram below to help you.

Person A: You want to buy a drill to do some home improvements. Ask the shop owner how to use one. How do you use it safely? Continually ask follow up questions.

Person B: Shop owner: You are an expert so you must answer all questions.

Role play:
Buying a Power Drill

Person A:
You want to buy a drill to do some home improvements.
Ask the shop owner how to use one.
How do you use it safely?
Continually ask follow up questions.

Person B:
Shop owner: Answer all questions.

Role Play

Repair Man

Person A: There are a few things that need repairing in your house. Phone a local repair man to do the work.

Person B: Repair man. Tell them how long the work will take, how you will do the work and what tools you will need, (you can use the vocabulary in all three worksheets to help you).

Finish Class

Additional Questions and Activities

1: Adjectives describing property
Think of some positive and negative ones. Some are opposites, such as old and modern, cramped and spacious.

2: BTQ: Describe the most stylish or worst looking building you ever visited.
What was the building? Where was it?
When did you go? Who with?
Why did you go there? Why did it stand out in our mind?

3: How could you make where you live look really modern?
This can be done even if students live in a dormitory. Have fun with it.

4: Think of three ways to improve the look of the classroom.

Roleplay

Change your family apartment
Person A: You are now a professional person almost 30 years old.
You think the apartment could look more modern.
Tell your parents you want to change it and how.
Person B: Parents. No way! You don't want to change anything.

Woodwork Teacher

Person A: You are the head teacher of a High School.
You need to hire a new woodwork teacher. Ask interview questions.
Person B: You are an expert carpenter.
Talk about your experience and how you can make your lessons both safe and interesting.
You can use the job interview questions found in Topic 14.

Job Interview

Person A: Go to a job interview at a local DIY store.
Talk about your experience and why you want the job.
Person B: Boss.
Ask job interview questions including how you use some of the tools.

Famous Designer

Person A: Famous designer.
You are well known across China on TV and in magazines.
Recently you changed Lin Zhi Ling's apartment in Taiwan. Talk about it on CCTV.
How did the apartment look before and after?
Person B: CCTV interviewer.
Continually ask follow up questions.

Vocabulary and useful expressions

Floor：地板, windows：窗, ceiling：天花板, walls：墙壁
Painting：绘画, decorating：装饰
Hand tools：手动工具, power tools：动力工具
Tin of paint：一罐油漆, roller：滚轴, brush：刷子, roller tray：滚压台
Screwdriver：螺丝刀, step ladder：梯子
Repair：修理
Hammer：锤子, nails：钉子, screws ：螺丝刀
Pliers：老虎钳, saw：锯, square：直角尺

Painting and Decorating

Match the numbers with the names

1

screw driver
tin of paint
roller
roller tray
step ladder
sander
paint brush

3

2

7

5

6

4

DIY Tools

Match the different tools with the numbers

screw driver   pliers   saw   nail
square   hammer
screw

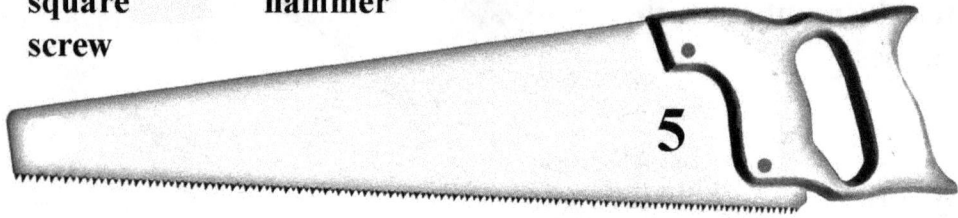

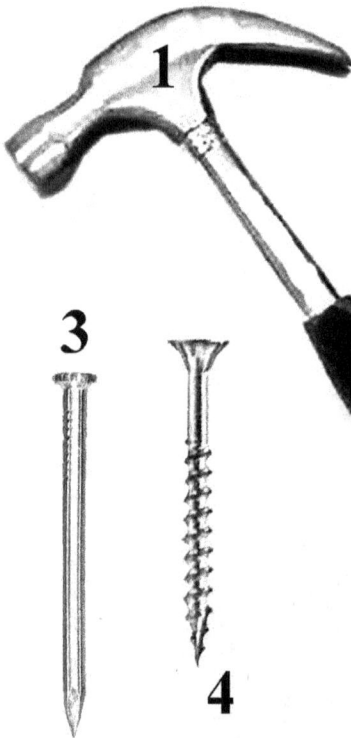

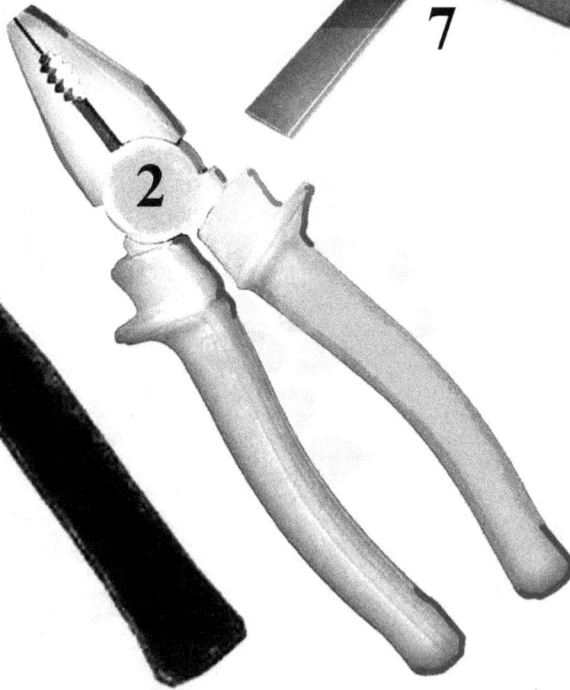

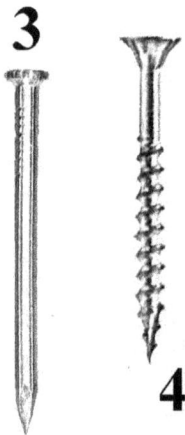

5

6

1

7

2

3

4

Power Drill

2: drill bit

1 & 3 chuck key

6

On/Off **7**

trigger **9**

6

5 safety goggles

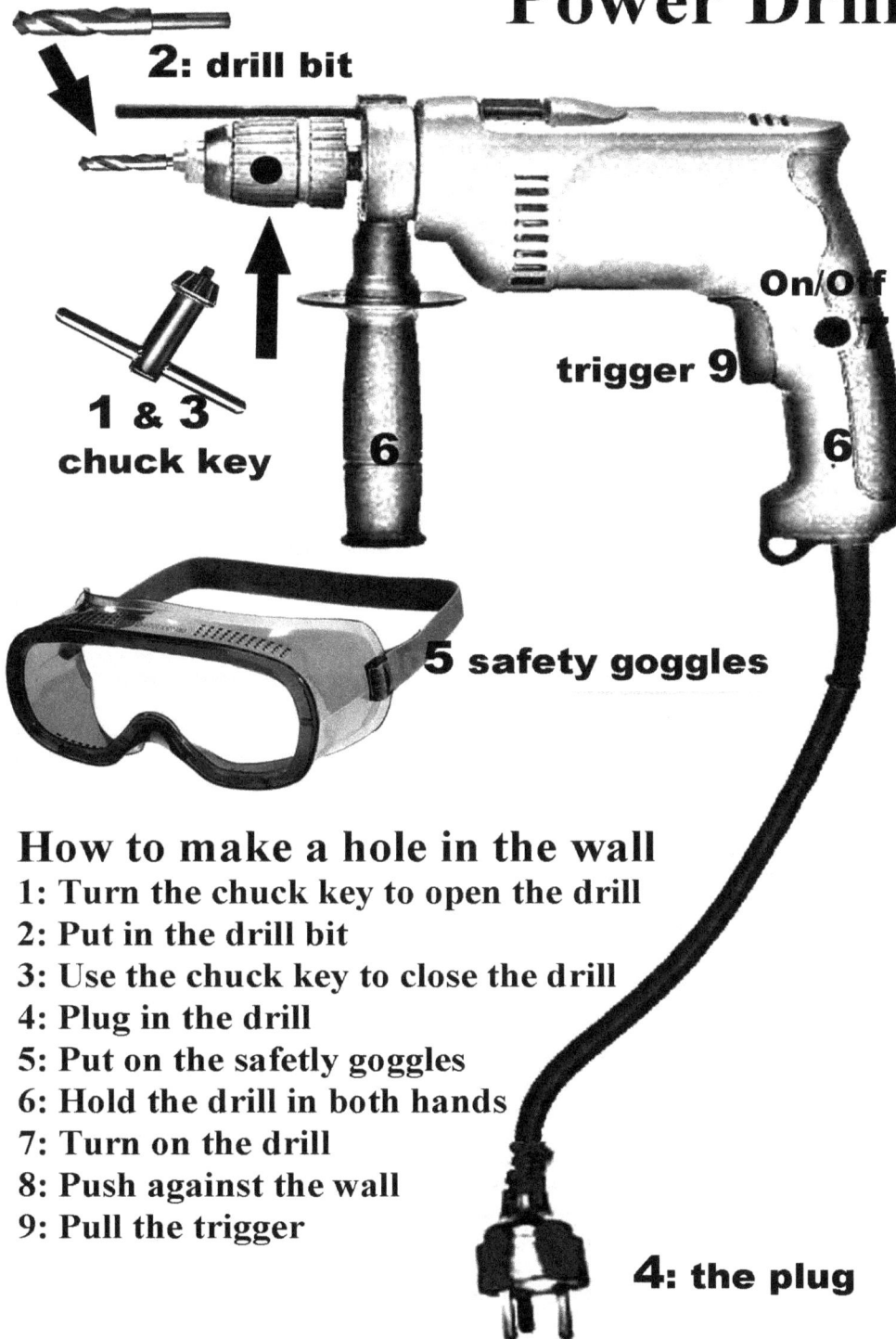

How to make a hole in the wall
1: Turn the chuck key to open the drill
2: Put in the drill bit
3: Use the chuck key to close the drill
4: Plug in the drill
5: Put on the safetly goggles
6: Hold the drill in both hands
7: Turn on the drill
8: Push against the wall
9: Pull the trigger

4: the plug

Topic
09 Festivals

Brainstorm Vocabulary

What do you know?

At the beginning of class, think of any vocabulary that you already know along with your classmates. If there is anything you don't know then <u>write it in the space below</u> and practice using it during class. Make sure you understand if it's a noun, verb, adjective or adverb. Make sure your pronunciation is accurate and that you know how to use it in a sentence. Is it formal or informal?

Write new vocabulary and expressions here:

Discussion

- When does the festival take place? What date?
- What is the meaning of the festival? Why do we have it?
- What special food is eaten then?
- What decorations are used?
- Are there any special stories that go with the festival?

1: Describe a Chinese festival.
Make sure you answer all the questions above.

2: Describe Christmas.
Make sure you answer all the questions above.
What happens on December 24th, 25th and the 26th?
What is the story of Christmas?

3: Describe a second Chinese Festival.
Again, use the questions above to help you.

4: Double Days
What are the various 'double days' in China? Describe them and their meaning.

5: Mother's Day (past tense)
What did you do for your Mum last Mother's Day?
What was the best thing you ever did for your Mum on Mother's Day?

6: New Festival
If you could create a new festival in China what would it be called?
When would it be? What would it be about?
You should briefly write your ideas down.

Devil's Advocate

We should forget festivals like Christmas and concentrate on Chinese traditions such as the Spring Festival.

Role Play

New Festival
Use the notes you made earlier for Q6.
If you finish early then change the roles.

<u>Person A:</u> You are a representative of the government. You have created a new festival that will be held throughout China. Proudly announce it live on CCTV.
<u>Person B:</u> CCTV interviewer. This is very exciting. Continually ask questions. Remember the questions used at the beginning of class.

Queue Jumper
<u>Person A:</u> It is the Spring Festival. You have been queuing at the train station for a ticket for three hours. You are tired, cold and hungry.
<u>Person B:</u> Queue jumper. You urgently need a ticket. Go to the front of the queue and buy your ticket. You must get it. Be persistent.
<u>Person A:</u> No way! Do not allow this person to push in front of you.

Finish Class

Additional Questions and Activities

1: Projector
Your teacher may show you photos of festivals in their country. Think about how different Western festivals are to Chinese ones.
Make sure you listen to them and ask questions. Don't sit quietly. Remember that even simple questions can be important.

2: How do you normally spend the Spring Festival?
How did you spend it last year? (past tense)

3: 2008 (past tense)
2008 was known as 'China's Year'. What happened to you during the Spring Festival that year? Did you travel by train? Tell your story. How about the rest of your family?

4: Valentine's Day
Think of five things you could do for your partner on Valentine's Day

5: Describe your best festival memory (past tense)
Was it during the Spring Festival? When was it? What made it special?

6: Spring Festival TV
In recent years CCTV has broadcast special TV throughout Spring Festival Eve and Spring Festival Day.
Do you watch it with your family or are you uninterested in it?
What do you like and dislike about the broadcast?

Devil's Advocate

We should only have one Valentine's Day and that should be the traditional Chinese one; Double Seven Day!

Role Play

Getting it right
Person A: You are a representative from the government. You have new plans for easing the transport problems in China for the next Chinese New Year. Talk about your plans on CCTV.
Person B: CCTV interviewer. It is a very difficult problem to solve. Continually ask follow up questions to anything they say.

Vocabulary and useful expressions

Full：完全的, half：一半的,
Crescent and dark moon：新月和暗月（看不见月亮的时期）
Lunar calendar：农历
Queue jumper：插队者
1st 2nd 3rd etc for pronunciation of dates：第一、第二、第三日等日期的读法
Equinox：昼夜平分点，春分或秋分

Transport

Focuses mainly on land transportation.

Brainstorm Vocabulary

What do you know?

At the beginning of class, think of any vocabulary that you already know along with your classmates. If there is anything you don't know then <u>write it in the space below</u> and practice using it during class. Make sure you understand if it's a noun, verb, adjective or adverb. Make sure your pronunciation is accurate and that you know how to use it in a sentence. Is it formal or informal?

Write new vocabulary and expressions here:

Discussion

1: Unpowered transport
Think of five modes of unpowered transport (having no engine).
Describe them with "A bicycle is a mode of transport that…" rather than giving a one word answer.

2: BTQ: **Describe your longest journey** (past tense)
Where was it, when and who with?
How long did it take?
Did you <u>transfer</u>? How many different modes of transport did you use? Why were you travelling?

3: Sleeper Trains
Have you ever travelled by sleeper train? Describe your journey. Did you enjoy it?
What are the advantages and disadvantages of travelling by sleeper train?

4: Give advice
If a foreigner who had never been to China before was travelling by sleeper train or bus, what three <u>tips</u> could you give them?

5: Cars
Which car would you most like to have? Why?
What <u>statement</u> would it make about you?
Example: A jeep tells people you are a tough and assertive outdoor person. Maybe you could say practical if you use it out of town.

6: Transport of the Future (future tense)
Describe what transport will be like in 50 years time.
Think about transport in cities, between cities and international travel.
Emphasize that this is the future tense and ask students to give examples of usage before they start.

Devil's Advocate

If you live in the city, buying a car is a waste of time. It's better to catch a taxi every day instead.

Role Play

Buy a second hand car

Part 1:
Fill in the worksheet called 'Cars' in the vocabulary and useful expressions section below.
Go through the different parts of a car with your teacher, for example, *wheels, doors and lights etc...*

Part 2:
You are buying a private car, not one from a company show room.
Person A: You want to buy a secondhand car. Ask this person questions about their car. Use the vocabulary from the list to help you.
Person B: You want to sell your family car. Why are you selling it? What have you been using it for?

Finish Class

Additional Questions and Activities

1: What are the most dangerous modes of transport?
Think of at least three.
You can also vote for the most dangerous in the list and explain why.

2: Think of five subway systems from around the world.
Which is the most impressive and why?

3: When the world runs out of oil what will our transport be like?
Think about transport in cities, between cities and international travel.
Remember that this is future tense.

4: Talk about the best bicycle you ever had (past tense)
If you have never had a bike before you can talk about your parent's or relative's.

Devil's Advocate

Each city should have a 'no drive zone' in the centre.
Instead people should be made to use public transport.

Roleplay

New Bicycle
Part 1:
Fill in the worksheet called 'My New Bicycle' in the vocabulary and useful expressions section below

Part 2:
Person A: You want to buy a new bike. Yours was recently stolen.
Person B: Shop owner. Try and sell your most expensive bike including accessories.

Driving Lessons (Upper Intermediate Level)

Part 1:
Label the worksheet called 'Car Interior' in the vocabulary and useful expressions section below.

Part 2:
In pairs work through the procedure for starting the car and moving forward.
Use the sequencing 'First, second, next and finally'.
Find the verbs and phrasal verbs in each sentence.

Part 3:
Person A: Driving Instructor.
You have a new student today.
Tell them about road safety, the procedure for starting the car and going forward.
Person B: Student.
You are very worried. This is your first time driving a car.
Continually ask follow up questions to the instructor.

Parking Space
Person A: Your neighbours continually park in your parking space outside your house.
It's really inconvenient and annoying.
Go to their house and ask them to move their car.
Person B: Neighbour.
You have two cars. You have to park it there. Make excuses not to move it.

Bad Driving
Person A: Traffic Police. You have caught that person driving too fast across a red light.
Your computer says this is the second time they have done this. You don't like drivers who drive too fast. Give them a heavy fine.
Person B: Driver. Make an excuse. Avoid paying the fine.

Company Car

Person A: Business partner. You want to buy a new company car for your business. You want to buy a small 'Smart Car' which will be cheaper and better for the environment.

Person B: Business partner. Disagree with your partner. You want to buy a large BMW as the company car.

Borrow your friend's car

Part 1

Person A: You really need to borrow your friend's car this weekend. Persistently ask to borrow it.

Person B: Make excuses not to lend it. You also need to use it.

Vocabulary and useful expressions

Mode of transport：运输方式

Train: 火车 engine：机车, carriage：客车, compartment：车厢,

Bunk bed：（附有梯子的）双层床

Bus：公共汽车, double decker：双层公共汽车, sleeper bus：卧铺客车,

Minibus：小型公共汽车（小巴）

Subway, London Underground, the Tube：地铁

Motorbike：摩托车, bike：摩托车, moped：机动脚踏两用车,

Electric bike：电动自行车, super bike：超级摩托车

Bicycle：自行车, bike：自行车, to cycle：骑自行车, tricycle：三轮车

Pillion：（摩托车等的）后座

Secondhand：用过的，二手的

Cars

Label the drawing with as many parts as you can. Some have already been done for you.

mirror

Wheels

My new bike

1: Add as many labels as you can
to this drawing.

2: Think of 5 things that are
missing from this bike.

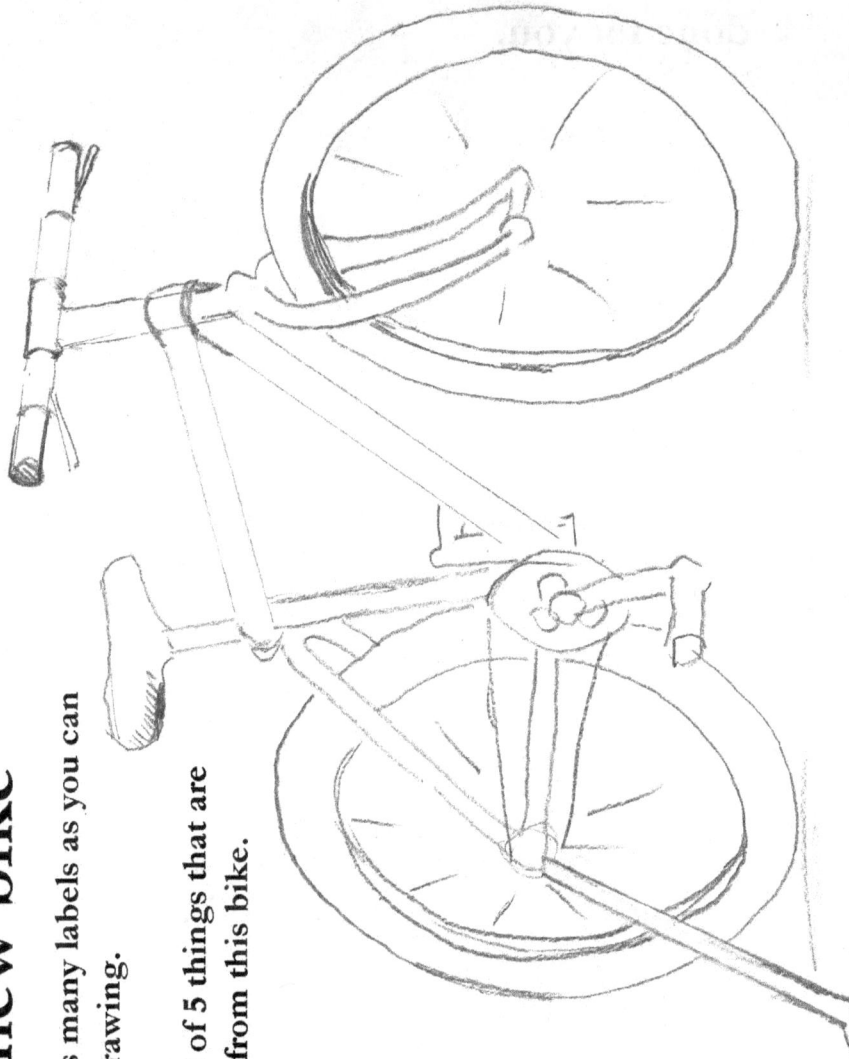

Car interior

Add as many labels as you can to this drawing. Two have already been done for you.

mirror

gear stick

Procedure for starting the car and moving forward.

1: Put on your safety belt
2: Put the key in the ignition
3: Make sure the car is in neutral gear
4: Turn the ignition and start the engine
5: Look in your mirrors
6: Press down the clutch pedal with your foot
7: Change into first gear using the gear lever
8: Make sure you have both hands on the steering wheel
9: Look in your mirrors
10: Slowly take your foot off the clutch pedal
11: With your other foot press down the accelerator
12: Congratulations. You are now driving!

Topic
11 Travel & Tourism

Brainstorm Vocabulary

What do you know?

At the beginning of class, think of any vocabulary that you already know along with your classmates. If there is anything you don't know then write it in the space below and practice using it during class. Make sure you understand if it's a noun, verb, adjective or adverb. Make sure your pronunciation is accurate and that you know how to use it in a sentence. Is it formal or informal?

Write new vocabulary and expressions here:

Discussion

1: Choose a Country
Work in pairs.
One student from each pair should take a card from the bag.
For the rest of the lesson, this will be your country. You and your classmate must collect as much information about your country as possible. This will be needed for the role play at the end of class.

Think of six key words to do with your country
For example, *China: Great Wall, Beijing, Shanghai, provinces, pandas, hot-pot*

2: Which country would you most like to visit? Why?
This means for interest or vacation, not just going somewhere because of college.

3: Would you like to go to the country you have chosen? Why or why not?
Think of at least three positive things about your country.

4: Would you like to arrange a package holiday with a travel agent?
Would you like to organize your holiday by yourself? Why or why not?

5: Map Work
Use the map of the world that your teacher has brought into class.
What information can you get to tell you about your country from the map?

Look at the map and write as much information down about the country you chose in Q1.

6: How do you like to travel? Why?
Also, which one don't you like? Why?

Independently
As part of a tour group
With a friend
With two friends
With your family
With your partner; gf/bf, husband/wife

7: BTQ: Describe the best holiday you went on (past tense)
Where did you go? When, who with and how did you get there? What was the food like, hotel and weather? What did you do there? Any special stories?

8: Where are the best and worst places to go on holiday in China? Why?

Role Play

Souvenir Shop
Work in groups of three or in pairs.
Person A: You own a small souvenir shop at the Great Wall. Sell your souvenirs to some foreign tourists. Tell them why your souvenirs are special.
Person B & C: Tourists. All these souvenirs look cheap. They are all the same. Why should you buy any of these?

Travel Agents
Use the information for the country you picked in Q1.

Group A: Travel Agents. Your boss has given you a special holiday (your country) to promote. Sell this holiday to some customers.
Whatever country they want to go to, return the conversation back to your promotion.

Use your notes to help you promote this holiday.

Group B: You are a family. You want to book a package holiday. Think of somewhere suitable. You don't like the one the travel agents are promoting.

Finish Class

Additional Questions and Activities

1: Which is your ideal holiday? Why?
Rest and relax
Outdoors and adventure
Visiting historic places
A combination
A hot or cold place
You are not allowed to say "Stay at home".

2: What are the advantages and disadvantages that tourism brings to an area?

3: Where do you want to go on your honeymoon? Why?

4: How would you prepare before going abroad?
Include important things you would need to take.

5: BTQ: **Talk about the best or worst hotel you ever stayed in.**
Where was it? Why were you staying there? When were you there? Who were you with? What was the food like? What was the service like? What was wrong with it? How much was it per night? (past tense) You can also talk about the best hotel instead.

Devil's Advocate

Tourism is terrible for the local environment.

Package holidays are terrible. Better to plan your own holiday.

Role Play

Bring tourism to your village
Work in small groups.
Group A: Villagers. You want to bring tourism to your village. You have an ancient history including an old temple.
This will be an excellent way for you to make money.
Group B: Villagers. You think it's a terrible idea. Tourism will destroy your wonderful village forever.
Key words: *pollution, rubbish, safety, noisy, damage property, strangers.*

Tour Bus
Work in small groups.
Person A: Tour guide on a tour bus. Tell the passengers that you will be stopping soon at a local souvenir shop. The bus will be stopping for one hour. They should buy a souvenir from the shop.
Person B & C: You think that the tour guide may be friends with the shop owner. You don't want to buy anything or waste one hour of your day. Complain!

Hotel: Itinerary
Work in small groups.
Person A: You are the manager of a five star hotel in town. Welcome your guests. Introduce them to some of your excellent world class facilities. You have also made an itinerary for them around town this weekend. It includes shopping, eating and visiting famous places.
Person B & C: Guests. You have special requirements. Also you are not happy with some of the services and the itinerary. Continually make changes.

Hotel: Alarm Call
Person A: You asked for an alarm call yesterday but it didn't happen this morning. As a result you were late for a meeting. You lost business and your boss is angry.
Complain to the staff you asked last night. Demand compensation.
Person B: Staff. You forgot but don't tell them. Make an excuse. It's not your fault.

Vocabulary and useful expressions

Travel agency：旅行社
Package holiday：（旅行社安排一切的）一揽子旅游,
Package tour：包办旅行（路线、地点、时间和费用等均作统一规定和安排的旅游）,
Itinerary：旅程
Tour guide：导游, tour party：旅游团, tourist：旅行者, too touristy：游客太多
Souvenir：纪念品
Five star hotel: 五星级酒店 guesthouse：高级宾馆, youth hostel：青年招待所,
B+B (Bed +Breakfast): B+B（床 +早餐）
Continent：大陆, southern, northern hemisphere：南、北半球
Equator：赤道

Topic
12 Studying Abroad

Brainstorm Vocabulary

What do you know?

At the beginning of class, think of any vocabulary that you already know along with your classmates. If there is anything you don't know then <u>write it in the space below</u> and practice using it during class. Make sure you understand if it is a noun, verb, adjective or adverb. Make sure your pronunciation is accurate and that you know how to use it in a sentence. Is it formal or informal?

Write new vocabulary and expressions here:

Discussion

1: Which country would you most like to go to for study?
Why did you choose it in place of other popular countries?
If you aren't going abroad to study then think of any country you would like to travel to and why?

2: BTQ: What do you know about the country you would like to study in?
or what do you know about the country you would most like to visit?

Think of:
Five cities in that country.
Two famous places. Describe them.
What the weather is like.
What the food is like.
Anything important you know about it.
Write your answers down.

You should describe the famous places, not give one word answers.

3: Culture Shock:
How do you think you would feel leaving your home country for a long time?
What would you miss about your country and your home?
What would you do to overcome culture shock?
What do you think reversed culture shock is? If you don't know have a guess.

4: Jet Lag
Your teacher will give a brief talk on what this is. If you are going to travel to another country you may get jet lag.

5: How would you prepare before leaving for another country?
What important things would you need to do before going?
What important things would you take?

6: What makes you feel most nervous about going to another country?

7: How do you think foreign campuses are different from Chinese ones?
Think of social life, night life, hobbies and interests, dating, ratio of work and relaxation.
How do you <u>imagine</u> life to be?

8: Language Survival
When you go to a new country what ways could you overcome the language barrier?
Most people will speak completely differently from slow paced text book English.

Role Play

Persuade your friend

Person A: You are a student on a Western campus. You have been invited out to a party, meeting at a bar beforehand. You don't want to go alone. Persuade your friend to go with you.

Person B: Friend. You are very shy. Make excuses not to go, for example, *too busy, don't like smoking, drinking, too noisy, dangerous, too late and don't like clubs.*

At a Party

You should use the notes you made in Q2. In this roleplay Person B will be from the country they chose in Q2.

Person A: Chinese student. You are at a party at your college in China. You have met a foreign student from (Q2). This is very exciting as you haven't met anyone from another country before. Continually ask them follow up questions about their home country.

Person B: You are from (Q2). Answer all the questions. You can't say "I don't know". If you don't know then make up an answer. You cannot ask any questions about China to Person A. You can only answer questions.

Foreign Partner

Work in twos or threes.

Person A: While studying abroad you found a foreign gf/bf. You have been living together for six months. Phone up your parents in China and tell them.

Person B (& C): Parent(s). You strongly don't approve of this. Insist that your son/daughter finishes this relationship.

Vocabulary and useful expressions

Embassy: 大使馆
Passport: 护照
Visa: 签证, entry: 入口, exit: 出口
Single, double and multi entry (visa): 一次入境，两次入境和多次入境签证
Culture shock: 文化冲击, reversed culture shock: 逆向文化冲突

Topic
13 Schools, Teachers & Education

Brainstorm Vocabulary

What do you know?

At the beginning of class, think of any vocabulary that you already know along with your classmates. If there is anything you don't know then write it in the space below and practice using it during class. Make sure you understand if it's a noun, verb, adjective or adverb. Make sure your pronunciation is accurate and that you know how to use it in a sentence. Is it formal or informal?

Write new vocabulary and expressions here:

Discussion

1: Would you <u>make</u> a good teacher? Why or why not?
Would you like to be a teacher?

2: What duties does a teacher have?
This is other than teaching. Think of five.

3: If you were a teacher, what would your teaching style be?
Would you be a <u>strict</u> teacher or a friendly teacher?
How would you arrange your classroom?
What subject would you like to teach and why?

4: Describe the best teacher you ever had (past tense)
What qualities did they have that made them a good teacher?

Describe your worst teacher (past tense)
What made then such a terrible teacher?

5: School Facilities
What facilities does a school will normally have?
Your teacher will make a list with you on the white board.

6: BTQ: Punishment (past tense)
Students will have no problem talking about this subject.
Were you punished at school? What for? What happened?
Think of three other types of punishment that are given at school.

7: BTQ: Cheating (past tense)
Did you cheat in an exam at school? Why did you do it? How did you do it? Were you successful? How often did you do it?
If you never cheated, what ways are there to cheat in exams?

Devil's Advocate

There should be a relaxed approach in schools by having no uniforms.

Role Play

New School
Use the vocabulary from the list you made in Q5.
Person A: Parent. You want your child to go to an excellent middle school. Talk to the head teacher and ask them questions about their school.
Person B: Head teacher: Promote your school and tell the parent about the excellent facilities you have, for example, "We have the most modern gym in the city. Our teachers are all ex Olympic specialists".

Parents' Evening
Person A: English & PE teacher. Meet with the parents. Tell them about their child's progress.
Give them some praise for two things.
Give them some criticism for two things, for example.
- They haven't done their homework lately.
- They have been badly behaved in class.
- They were late.
- They had poor exam results.

Blame the parents for one of these and make a suggestion to them.
Think of a plan to make improvements.

Person B: Parents. You think the teacher should do more to help your child, not you.

Finish Class

Additional Questions and Activities

1: What were you favourite/ least favourite subjects at school? Why? (past tense)

2: Should a teacher be a student's friend? Why or why not?

3: Best Friend (past tense)
Talk about your best friend from school. Tell a story about something you did together.

4: Bullying
If you were a teacher and you found that one of your students was being bullied, what would you do?

5: The Education System
What is your opinion of the education system in China?
Could you make any improvements?

Devil's Advocate

There should be fewer tests and exams at school.

There should be more school trips to interesting places.

Dating should not be encouraged at school.

Cooking should be taught in school.

Role Play

School outdoor activities weekend
Person A: Teacher.
You have arranged an outdoor activities weekend for the kids.
They are between 8 and 10 years old.
Tell the parents your plans for the weekend.
Key words: *camping, hiking, collecting things, drawing and horse riding.*

Person B: Parent.
Of course you are worried about your child going away for the first time.
Continually ask the teacher questions:
Key words: *safety, weather, food, transport, where will they stay?*

Interview
Person A: Head teacher.
Your school needs a new teacher (choose any subject).
Interview this person for the job.
Ask questions about their experience etc.

Person B: Teacher.
How will you make your lessons interesting?
Talk about your teaching methods.
Talk about your high standards of student achievement.

Vocabulary and useful expressions

In China, education is referred to in American English. Middle school ages range from 11-13 and in high school ages range from 14-18. (Also US).
Secondary/Comprehensive: The UK's main form of education from 11-18.

Head teacher：校长
Curriculum：课程
Extra curricular activities：课外活动
Math (US), maths (UK)：数学
Core subject：核心课程
Compulsory：必修的
Prep work：准备工作
Invigilation：监考
Strict：严格的
Bully：恐吓
Teacher's pet：老师的得意门生
Excluded：排除的, suspended：暂停的
Truant, bunking off (UK): 逃学

Topic
14 Jobs & in the Office

Brainstorm Vocabulary

What do you know?

At the beginning of class, think of any vocabulary that you already know along with your classmates. If there is anything you don't know then <u>write it in the space below</u> and practice using it during class. Make sure you understand if it is a noun, verb, adjective or adverb. Make sure your pronunciation is accurate and that you know how to use it in a sentence. Is it formal or informal?

Write new vocabulary and expressions here:

Discussion

1: Write down three interview questions.
The questions should be the most likely ones to be asked in an interview.
People never ask about your name or qualifications as it will be on the application form.
Salary is often not mentioned in an interview.
Work with a partner and make your three sentences as grammatically accurate as possible.
You can use these when you go to a real interview.

2: What are your working strengths?
Think of at least three things you are good at.

3: Stress
Which jobs are the most stressful? Why?
Talk about a stressful time in your life? How did you overcome the stress? (past tense)

4: Management
Would you like to be a manager? Why or why not?
Would you <u>make</u> a good manager? Describe the duties of a manager. Think of four.

5: Stationary
Write down ten types of stationary when the teacher says 'Go!'
The first person to get to ten should call out or put up their hand.

Devil's Advocate

All managers should have a degree, major or masters in this area.
Non-qualified people should not be managers.

Role Play

Job Interview Practice
Work in groups of three or pairs.
Use this time practicing answering the interview questions.

<u>Person A:</u> Go for a job interview for _____. Answer all the questions.
<u>Person B & C:</u> Bosses: Ask interview questions. Ask follow up questions.

Fired from their last job

Person A: You were fired from your last job. Attend an interview for a new job
Try and avoid any questions about your previous work.

Person B: Boss. Ask the interview questions. A colleague told you they heard this person was fired. Ask the candidate why they left their last position?

Finish Class

Additional Questions and Activities

1: Describe your ideal job.
Think of three things that you would most like to have in your contract, for example, *flexi-time, work at home, work out of the office, benefits and a company car.*

2: Overtime
If you were asked in an interview whether you were able to work in the evenings and at the weekends what would you say? How about Sunday mornings?
If you are already working, how much overtime do you do? Do you get paid for it?

3: Meetings
Do you like meetings? Why or why not?
Why do companies have meetings?
What are important things to consider when arranging a meeting?

Devil's Advocate

People dress far too casually at work these days with t-shirts, jeans and sports shoes.
Staff should take pride in their company and therefore their appearance.

You should not be able to use the internet for personal reasons at work.

Role Play

Overbearing Employee
Person A: Boss. You have had complaints that your new employee is irritating in the office. They are too chatty and loud. They don't take the job seriously. Tell them they must change their behaviour immediately.
Person B: Employee. Defend yourself.

Unable to get a job
Person A: You are 45 and have been unemployed for six months. Go to a job interview for an office job. You must get this job.
Person B: Boss. You have lots of younger people who want the job. Why should you give the job to this person?

College Graduate
Person A: You left college six months ago. You have been unable to get a job as there are so many others going for the same position. Go to a job interview for an office job. You must get this job.
Person B: Boss. You have many others who want the job. Why should you give the job to this person? What outstanding qualities do they have?

Negotiating a pay rise
Person A: Manager. You are Irritated and slightly annoyed by this employee
You don't like this employee.
They are often late.
They are often on their mobile phone for personal calls.
They don't complete tasks on time.

You don't like that this employee is the other managers relative.
You think they get special treatment and should be treated equally like all the other staff.

Person B: Manager. You are caring and sympathetic to your employee.
This employee is your relative. You know the pressures they have in their life.
However, recently their standards of work have dropped.
They are often late.
They are often on their mobile phone for personal calls.
They don't complete tasks on time.

Think of ways to help your employee.

Person C: Employee. You are depressed and stressed out
Recently you have had some great pressure in your life.
Your boss A is giving you too much work.
The company moved to a new office which is far away from your apartment.
However, your husband/wife has said that you need to be earning more money.
You have been at the company for 3 years. All other staff have had a pay-rise but not you.

Your Boss B will help you. He is one of your relatives.

Negotiate a pay increase.

Company Car

Person A: Business partner. You want to buy a new company car for your business. You want to buy a small 'Smart Car' which will be cheaper and better for the environment.

Person B: Business partner. Disagree with your partner. You want to buy a large BMW as the company car.

Interview debrief

Some companies will give you feedback on how you did in your interview.

After the interview questions in the main lesson plan, allow five minutes for the bosses to give some objective criticism on how the candidate could improve their interview technique.

Person A: Boss. The candidate for the interview was not successful. Give them some indication of what went wrong for them.

Person B: Candidate. Choose to take the criticism 'on board' or disagree with some points.

Vocabulary and useful expressions

Chief Exec': 首席执行官, manager: 经理, supervisor: 监督人,
Team leader: 组长，团队领导
Staff: 全体职员, P.A. (Personal assistant): 私人助理, secretary: 秘书, typist: 打字员,
receptionist: 接待员, temp': 临时雇员
Accountant: 会计人员, clerk: 职员 executive: 经理主管人员
Team: 团队, team member: 队员, team player: 有团队精神的人,
Part of the team: 团队的一员, team spirit: 团队精神
White collar worker: 白领工人, Manual worker: 体力劳动者,
Skilled: 熟练的, semi-skilled: 半熟练的, unskilled: 不熟练的
Career: 事业, new challenges: 新的挑战, new horizons: 新视野
Work load: 工作负载, multi-tasking: 多重任务, admin': 管理
Over time: 超时, flexi-time: 可伸缩的劳动时间（弹性工作制）
Self-critical: 律己严格的
Stationary : 固定的
Delegate: 代表
Take a back seat: <美>黯然引退，退居二线
Take it on board: 纳入考虑范围，列入议事日程
The big picture: （非正式）整体情况
Climb the ladder, work your way up the ladder: 以自己的方式攀登职业的阶梯

Job Interview Questions:

These questions are usually asked at any job interview.

Some are 'trick questions' (**TQs**) as they must be answered very carefully. The best answers are also given with a trick question.

1: Why did you choose our company?

2: Tell us a bit more about your experience.
They will already know your working history, but they may want you to go into more detail at the interview.

3: TQ: for a manager's job.
If you get the job, what changes would you make in the office/company?
The best answer for this is to say that you will not make any immediate changes. You will first observe how things are done before making any changes.

4: TQ: What are your strengths and weaknesses when you are at work?
For weaknesses the best answer you can give is that you think you are too <u>self-critical</u>. This means you find fault in what you do too much. Never be honest when you answer this question, for example, "Sometimes I forget some small details when completing a task".

5: TQ Do you prefer working independently or as part of a team?
It is best if you say that you like both. Give the reasons why you enjoy both ways of working.

6: Are you prepared to work <u>over-time</u> for us in the evenings and weekends?
Of course you have to say yes.

7: TQ: Why did you leave your last job?
Be careful. You can't say anything negative. The best answers are that you lived too far away from the office or you needed new challenges.

Brainstorm Vocabulary

What do you know?

At the beginning of class, think of any vocabulary that you already know along with your classmates. If there is anything you don't know then <u>write it in the space below</u> and practice using it during class. Make sure you understand if it is a noun, verb, adjective or adverb. Make sure your pronunciation is accurate and that you know how to use it in a sentence. Is it formal or informal?

Write new vocabulary and expressions here:

Discussion

1: BTQ: If you have lost your job life can be very difficult.
What effect does it have on someone when they lose their job?
What are the social effects of losing your job?

Talk about someone you know who lost their job. What happened?
How long did it take for them to get another job? (past tense)

2: In what ways can your job become difficult?
There are many ways in which an employee can become dissatisfied and stressed out at work. Think of and describe three ways.

3: Think of five reasons to fire someone
Which of these would warrant <u>immediate</u> dismissal? Why?

4: If you were a manager and an employee was late what would you do?
What about if they were late a second time?
How about if they were continually late?
How would you go about doing it?

5: If you had to <u>downsize</u> your company, which employees would you <u>lay off</u> first and why?

6: Finding a job
The unemployment rate is very high these days.
Why is it so difficult to find a job?
Think of three tips to improve your chances of getting a job.

Devil's Advocate

The government should do more to help the unemployed

Role Play

Appraisal

<u>Person A:</u> Manager. Give your employee their monthly appraisal. They are a secretary in the office. Give them both positive and negative things about their recent performance.

<u>Person B:</u> Employee. You have a few problems at work (use examples from Q2). Tell your manager and ask them for advice.

Downsizing

<u>Person A:</u> Boss. You need to make your company smaller. You are not making any money at the moment. Times are difficult.

Call your newest employee into the office and tell them that you are going to have to make them redundant. You are very sorry but there is nothing that you can do about it.

<u>Person B:</u> Employee. You have only been at the company for a few months. It took you a long time to get this job and you were unemployed for a long time before. Your wife/ husband will be really upset. Try and negotiate with your boss and keep your job.

Warning or Dismissal?
Give a warning

<u>Person A:</u> Boss. You have told your employee a two times about their negative behaviour (use examples from Q3). You have already given them two verbal warnings. Give them a final written warning.

<u>Person B:</u> Employee. Totally disagree with your boss. They are being really unfair. You have made some improvement lately. You think they just don't like you.

Vocabulary and useful expressions

Appraisal：评价
Probationary period：试用期间
Verbal warning：口头警告, written warning：书面警告
Downsize, streamline：裁减人数
Make redundant：裁员, lay-off：失业期
Fire, the sack, instant dismissal：解雇
Leave：休假, quit：辞职, walk out：罢工
Retire：退休

Topic

16 Telephoning

Brainstorm Vocabulary

What do you know?

At the beginning of class, think of any vocabulary that you already know along with your classmates. If there is anything you don't know then <u>write it in the space below</u> and practice using it during class. Make sure you understand if it's a noun, verb, adjective or adverb. Make sure your pronunciation is accurate and that you know how to use it in a sentence. Is it formal or informal?

Write new vocabulary and expressions here:

Discussion

1: How many phones have you owned? (past tense)
What happened to them? Did you break or lose them? Did you change your old phone?
How come? Which was the best?

2: Think of five <u>brands</u> of phone.
Which country are they from?

3: Making a friendly call (*see below*)
Its common in Western countries to call people on their <u>land-line</u> as it is still much
cheaper than phoning them on their mobile.

Work with your teacher on the white board practicing what someone might say when
making an informal-friendly call.
Pay attention to some of the tones in important words. Try not to speak in flat tones.

Practice with a partner for a few minutes.

4: What is your telephone number?
Say it in quick spoken English.

5: What will phones be like in 50 years' time? (future tense)
Remember to speak in the future tense.

6: Making a formal business call
Work with your teacher on the white board practicing what someone might say when
making a formal business call to a company.
Again, pay attention to some of the tones in important words.
Practice with a partner for a few minutes.

Role Play

Only an acquaintance
<u>Person A:</u> You are new in town. You don't have any friends and are lonely. However,
yesterday you met someone in a coffee shop and got their telephone number. '<u>Phone
them up</u>' and ask them to join you for lunch sometime. Be persistent. If they are busy
think of another time.
<u>Person B:</u> You don't really know this person and <u>regret</u> giving them your telephone
number. Make excuses not to meet them.

Sell your product

Person A: You are a sales representative. You sell computers and printers. You think this company may be interested in buying some. Phone them up. Introduce yourself and what you do. Ask to speak to the manager. You met them at a meeting last week and they gave you their business card.

Person B: Receptionist. Tell them that your manager is unavailable. Ask if they want to leave a message. Tell them when it will be convenient to call back.

Finish Class

Additional Questions and Activities

1: Smart Phones
How important is it for you to have the latest Smartphone? Why? Maybe you just want a phone to call someone or send messages? Which is the best Smartphone and why?

2: Which would you rather lose?
Your wallet or your mobile phone? Why?

3: What's the best thing about your phone?
What are the best functions? What is the worst thing about your phone?

4: Describe your ideal phone.

5: When is it bad manners to use your mobile phone?
Give three examples.
Do you ever use your phone when you know you shouldn't? When?

7: What are the advantages and disadvantages of mobile phones?
When do you turn your phone off and for how long?

8: What is the longest you have been without your phone? (past tense)
How long was it for and why? Where were you at the time?

9: Do you use the internet on your phone?
Which websites? How long do you spend on them?

Devil's Advocate

You should switch off your phone in the cinema.

Children should not be allowed mobile phones.

There should be strict laws against people who drive and use their mobile phone at the same time.

Role Play

Buy a new phone
Person A: You want to buy a new phone.
Person B: Shop assistant. Sell them your most expensive phone. Tell them about all the great new functions it has.

Pizza delivery driver
Person A: You ordered a pizza to be delivered to your apartment over two hours ago. You already phoned the shop, but it has still not arrived. Phone again and ask what has happened. Be angry.
Person B: You work in the restaurant. Answer the phone and make excuses why the pizza has still not been delivered.

Please be quiet!
Person A: You are working on your thesis in the library. That person keeps talking loudly on their mobile phone. Ask them to keep quiet.
Person B: Make excuses to keep using your phone.

Ask your parents
Person A: You are 15 years old and you want a cell phone. All your friends have one. Ask your parents. Be persistent.
Person B: Parent. Not yet. They are too young. Maybe next year.

Vocabulary and useful expressions

Cell phone, mobile phone, my mobile': 手机
Landline：陆上通讯[运输]线
Signal, reception, bars：信号
Credit：信誉, functions：功能
Public phones, pay phones, phone box, booth：公用电话
Area code：地区代码, international dialing code：国际拨号代码
Dial：拨打电话, engaged：电话占线, ring tone：电话铃音
Free numbers, emergency services, operator services
Reversed charges, collect call：对方付费电话
Phone up, call, bell someone：给某人打电话
Put you on hold： （电话）不要挂机,
Connect you, transfer you, put you through：转接电话

Calling your friend at home:

Mother: Hello?
          (tone: often rising to create a question)
You   : Hi, this is (you). Is Barry in please?
          (tone: 'please' can drop down and then rise again at the end)
Mother: Sure. Hold on while I go and get him.

or

Mother: Hello?
You   : Hi, this is (you). Is Barry in please?
Mother: Oh, he's not in at the moment. Do you want to leave
          a message?
You   : Yes please. Could you ask him to phone me when he
          gets back please?
Mother: Sure. No problem.
You   : Great. Thanks very much.
Mother: Bye
You   : Bye

or

Mother: Oh, he's not in at the moment. Can I take a
message?

Calling a client in their office:

Receptionist: Hello, this is Smart English.
(tone: 'hello' would be bright and cheerful)
How can I help?
(tone: the whole sentence starts high and drops down to the word 'help')

You   : Hello, could I speak to Mr Kirby in Sales please? (the sales department)

Receptionist: Fine. Hold on while I put you through.

or

Receptionist: Fine. I just need to put you on hold while I put you through.

or

Receptionist: Fine. I'll just transfer your call.

Receptionist 2: Hello, Sales. Who's speaking please?

You   : Hello. This is Mr/Mrs.......Could I speak to Mr Kirby please?

Receptionist 2: Could you hold on while I see if he is available?

You   : That's fine.

Possible Answer:

Receptionist 2: Hello. I'm sorry but he's not available at the moment.
Would you like to leave a message?

Topic
17 Books & Literature

Brainstorm Vocabulary

What do you know?

At the beginning of class, think of any vocabulary that you already know along with your classmates. If there is anything you don't know then <u>write it in the space below</u> and practice using it during class. Make sure you understand if it's a noun, verb, adjective or adverb. Make sure your pronunciation is accurate and that you know how to use it in a sentence. Is it formal or informal?

Write new vocabulary and expressions here:

Discussion

1: Think of six genres
Work with a partner for two minutes.

2: Think of five key words to use with horror.
What is the difference between a thriller and horror?

3: What important things make a good novel?

4: BTQ: **Recommend a great book.**
You can describe a situation in either the past or present tense.
The present tense can be very effective in keeping things exciting.
People often use the present tense to describe books or films.

Why is it a great book?
Why should we read it?
Describe what happens in the book.

You may not read anything except text books. If you find this question difficult then recommend a film. All films have a script. If you have an IELTS or TOEFL test and you are asked about books, this is an alternative way to answer.

5: If you were a writer
You should work individually and write this down.
If you were a writer writing your own book what genre would it be?
Think of a title for it. If you have time, think about what the plot may be about.
Keep it simple. Don't think too long about it.

6: Do you prefer fiction or non-fiction? Why?

Devil's Advocate

Books will be thing of the past.
We can get everything we need from the internet these days.

Role Play

Book Shop
Work in groups of three.
Person A: Book shop owner.
You have a small book shop. You don't make much money.
However, recently you noticed that your customers are only reading the books and never buying anything.
Make them buy a book.
Person B & C: Customers. Think of excuses not to buy anything.

Author
Work in groups of three.
Use the notes you made in Q5
Part 1: Literary Agent
Person A: You are a writer. You have just finished your first book.
Attend an interview with a literary agent and try to get a contract.
Use your notes from earlier; your genre and title of your book.
Talk about your book; the plot, why you wrote it etc.
Person B & C: Literary agents: Ask the write questions.
Why is this book different from other books of the same genre?
Why should they be interested in this book?

Part 2: Book Signing
Change roles. Get another classmate in your group to be the author.
Person A: Congratulations! Your book is a big success. It is a best seller.
Attend a book signing at a bookshop and meet your fans.
Person B & C: Fans. You love this book. You love this author and their style of writing.
You are very excited. Continually ask them questions such as:
Where do they get their ideas from?
What will they write next?
Why did they want to be a writer?
Why did they choose this genre?
Will they ever change genres?

Finish Class

Additional Questions and Activities

1: What are the greatest books in China?
Why are they so important?

2: What was the last book you read?
When did you read it and why?

3: Talk about a book you remember reading as a child?
Describe it. Why can you remember it?

4: E-books
E-books are becoming increasingly popular. What are their advantages and disadvantages?
Do you think they will replace regular books in the future?

5: What is the difference between Sci-Fi and Fantasy?

Devil's Advocate

Magazines are a waste of resources.
We should reduce the number of magazines produced to help save the environment.
No one reads a magazine properly anyway.

Roleplay

Children's Books
Person A: You want to buy a book as a birthday present for your friend's 6 year old child.
Person B: Shop assistant. Recommend something suitable.

Library Assistant:
Person A: Attend a job interview for a library assistant.
Person B: Curator: Ask interview questions.
You can use the interview questions in T34: Jobs & in the Office
Why are they interested in the job?
Talk about the different genres of book that really interest them.

Please be quiet!
Person A: You are working on your thesis in the library. That person keeps talking loudly on their mobile phone. Ask them to keep quiet.
Person B: Make excuses to keep using your phone.

Vocabulary and useful expressions

Writer, author：作者
Proofreader：校对者, editor：编辑, literary agent：文学经纪人, publisher：出版商
Manuscript：手稿
Hard back：精装本, soft back：平装书
E-book：电子书
Best seller：畅销书, book signing：签名售书
Fiction, non-fiction：小说，非小说类
Genre：体裁
Biography：传记, autobiography：自传
Plot：（戏剧、小说等的）情节, sub-plot：（戏剧、小说等的）次要情节
Browse, thumb, flick through：浏览

Topic

18 Languages

Brainstorm Vocabulary

What do you know?

At the beginning of class, think of any vocabulary that you already know along with your classmates. If there is anything you don't know then <u>write it in the space below</u> and practice using it during class. Make sure you understand if it is a noun, verb, adjective or adverb. Make sure your pronunciation is accurate and that you know how to use it in a sentence. Is it formal or informal?

Write new vocabulary and expressions here:

Discussion

1: Think of a country
One student (A) thinks of a country.
Their neighbour (B) must think of the language that is used there.
Student B now thinks of a country and their neighbour (C) must think of the language.
The activity travels around the class from classmate to classmate.

2: New Language
If you had to choose another language to learn, what would it be and why?

3: Think of:
8 places that speak English
5 countries that also speak Chinese
4 countries that speak Spanish
3 countries that speak French
2 countries that places Portuguese

4: LANGUAGES QUESTIONNAIRE

Portuguese, Dutch, Spanish, English, French, Arabic, Chinese, German

Which country uses which language? Choose from the list of languages from above.

1: Austria

2: Belgium

3: Brazil

4: Cameroon

5: Egypt:

6: Iraq:

7: Ireland:

8: Netherlands:

9: Singapore:

10: Mexico:

4: Language acquisition
Think of five tips you could give a friend who wanted to start learning English.

5: European Sounds
This is to give you an idea of some of the most common European pronunciations.

Your teacher will write some sentences on the white board.
Which European country do these sentences belong to?
What do you think they mean? Guessing meanings of individual words is helpful.
Try and say each sentence.

6: Forms of Connected Speech
Spoken English is completely different from written-text book English.
Often important letters in each word are either changed of replaced.

Assimilation:
The letters /**d, t and n**/ are changed before the start of a second word
Change the following words and phrases into spoken English

1: Good Morning
2: Ten Pounds
3: Hot potato
4: Not quite
5: Good girl

Elision: Removing /d & t/
Often the letters d and t are removed.
Pronounce the following words without the d or t:

Hand bag, Old man, Used to, Last week, Most people, Act sensibly, Software, You and me, Where and why?

Catenation:
This is where one or more words join with the next word. Often this will sound like one long word rather than separate words which can be really confusing for non-native speakers

Please come here.
He kicked his football.
He fell on the ground.
Your socks need a wash.
Remember to buy an onion.
Get off the sofa and take your shoes off.

Weak forms
These are structure words that can be said in two ways. This allows us to talk faster than keeping the sounds the same as textbook English. Change the following sentences into spoken English:

1: Go to the shops and buy some apples.
2: Have you got the time please?
3: Can I watch the TV tonight or are you going to use it?

Devil's Advocate

We should learn the languages of our neighbouring countries such as Japanese and Korean as well as learning English.

Role Play

Language Teacher
Person A: Head teacher.
You need a new language teacher. Interview someone for the job. Ask interview questions such as what is your experience? Why our School? How many languages can you speak? Why are you interested in languages?
You can also use the questions found in T34: Jobs & in the Office.
Person B: Teacher. How can you make your lessons interesting? How can you get successful exam results?

Finish Class

Additional Questions and Activities

1: BTQ: When you were at school (past tense)
When you were at school how did they teach English? What were their methods? Did you like this learning style? Why or why not? Think of four ways to improve on the system.

2: Word Association

When your classmate says one word what do you <u>associate</u> with it?

For example, if they said 'green' you may reply 'tree, plant, new, sick, red, colour,' and so on. Whatever you say, the classmate on your other side must then think of a word which associates with it. This will then continue quickly around the class.

There are only three rules for this

- If you repeat what someone else has said then YOU ARE OUT!
- If you wait/pause for longer than 10 seconds then YOU ARE OUT!
- No helping classmates.

The last person is the winner.

3: Heteronyms

These are words that share the same spelling but have different pronunciations with strong sounds, for example, 'p<u>e</u>rmit' is a noun and 'perm<u>i</u>t' is a verb.

Underline the strong sounds and think of the two meanings for each of these words:
convict, console, perfect, rebel, conduct, contract and *project*.

4: Stress in Sentences

If we stress certain words the meaning of a sentence can change.
What are the different meanings of each of these sentences? Write down your answers.
The strong sounds are underlined

A: <u>I'll</u> buy you a coffee.
B: I'll <u>buy</u> you a coffee.
C: I'll buy <u>you</u> a coffee.
D: I'll buy you a <u>coffee</u>.
E: I'll buy you <u>a</u> coffee.

Practice saying each one.

5: Schwa sounds

The vowel in a weak form is usually the schwa /ə/ in phonetic script.

Schwa sounds can be found within a single word as well as in weak forms, for example:

c<u>o</u>me here - cəme here

fath<u>e</u>r - fathər

f<u>o</u>r me - fər me

C<u>a</u>n you? - Cən you?

t<u>o</u>night - tənight

Practice pronouncing these with your teacher.

6: British English vs American English
Think of five examples where the vocabulary is different for the same thing.
For example
'trousers' is British English and 'pants' American English.
Be careful; 'pants' means 'underwear' in Britsh English.

Think of five differences in pronunciation
For example
Tomato: to**mar**to (British):   to**mayd**o (American)

7: Body language
Think of 4 ways we use our eyes to communicate.
Think of 4 ways we use our forehead to communicate.
Think of 4 ways we use our body to communicate.
Think of 8 ways we use our hands to communicate.
Which are rude? Which can be important?

Role Play

Tour Guide
Think of some useful phrases you would need if you were a tourist in a new country, for example
"Excuse me. Could you tell me how to get to the museum please?"
"How much is it please?", "Thank you very much." "What time is it please?"

Work in small groups
Person A: You are an English tour guide. You are in charge of some Chinese tourists who arrived today. They can't speak much English. Give them some advice, useful phrases and pronunciation. Correct their mistakes. Make them repeat it a few times.
Person B: Tourists: You find English very difficult, especially on pronunciation. Continually make mistakes and make the tour guide correct you.

Vocabulary and useful expressions

Bi-lingual, multi-lingual：双语、多语种
Second language：第二语言
Accent 重音: *a manner of pronunciation peculiar to a particular individual, location, or nation. An accent may identify the locality in which its speakers reside.*
Dialect 语调: *The term is applied most often to regional speech patterns, but a dialect may also be defined by other factors, such as social class.*
Connected Speech：连音, assimilation：同化, catenation：连锁, weak forms：弱读

19 Music

Brainstorm Vocabulary

What do you know?

At the beginning of class, think of any vocabulary that you already know along with your classmates. If there is anything you don't know then <u>write it in the space below</u> and practice using it during class. Make sure you understand if it is a noun, verb, adjective or adverb. Make sure your pronunciation is accurate and that you know how to use it in a sentence. Is it formal or informal?

Write new vocabulary and expressions here:

Discussion

1: Think of six genres of music. Describe two of them.
Work in pairs discuss for two minutes.

2: Talk about a song you can remember as a child (past tense)
Also, talk about the first song you really loved as a teenager.

3: BTQ: **Recommend some music that you really like now.**
What genre is it? Why do you like it? Is it the vocalist? Maybe it's the lyrics or their voice? How does it make you feel?

4: Instruments
What different types of musical instrument do you know? Work with your teacher.

5: Choose an instrument
If you could choose one musical instrument to start learning to play, what would it be and why?

6: Musicians in a band
What do you call the different musicians in a band? Work with your teacher.

7: Miming
What is your opinion of people who mime at a <u>live</u> concert? It may also be on TV. Would you pay for a ticket if you knew they were going to mime? Why do people mime?

8: How do you play the violin?
Go to 'Vocabulary and Useful Expressions' and label the violin worksheet.
Have a guess if you don't know and work with your teacher.

Use simple verbs and sequencing to describe how to play the violin:
'First you hold the bow in your left hand. Then, next' and 'finally' etc.
Keep it simple!

Devil's Advocate

We should learn about modern music at school as well as classical music.

Role Play

Form a band
Work in groups of three or four.
Congratulations. Your group is now in a band.
You need one person in your group to write everything down.
1: You should decide on the name of your band.
2: You should decide on the genre of your band.
3: You should decide on what each member of the band does including having a vocalist.
4: Write the name and first line of your first song. .

Finish Class

Additional Questions and Activities

1: Which musical genre don't you like? Why?
How does it make you feel?

2: How has music influenced fashion?
Think of some genres that are linked to fashion.
Think of the examples of how people dress according to the music they listen to, for example, people who listen to heavy metal often wear black t-shirts and leather jackets.
Men may grow their hair long.

3: Strong Language
What is your opinion of music which uses strong language?
Should it be banned?
Should it have a rating like there are with films?

4: Talk about a musician that you admire?
Why are they so great?

5: What is your opinion of musicians that take drugs?

6: What do your parents like to listen to?
Do you like it or does it hurt your ears?

7: BTQ: **Live Concert** (past tense)
Talk about a live concert or show that you went to.
Which band or who was it you went to see?
When and where?
Who did you go with?
What happened?
Did you enjoy it?
Was it indoor or outdoor?

Devil's Advocate

I love Michael Jackson

We should play more Western music on radio and TV

Roleplay

Live Concert
Person A: You want to go to see your favourite band at a concert tonight. You don't want to go alone. Invite your friend to go. You have already bought the tickets.
Person B: You would rather watch it on TV. It's much more convenient that way.

Form a Band – Variations
These can be added on to the roleplay in the main lesson plan.

Record Contract
Group A: Band: Your group needs a recording contract. Go and see a famous producer and try and get a contract.
Group B: Record Producers: You interview many new bands. Why is this band different? Why are they special? Why do they think they will become famous?
Ask interview questions such as why did they want to be in a band? Where do they get their ideas from?

Meet your fans
Group A: Fans. You are absolutely crazy about this band. You love them so much. Now is your chance to meet them and ask them as many questions as you can. You can ask them anything.
Group B: Band. Answer all the questions. If there is anything embarrassing, get another band member to answer it.

Vocabulary and useful expressions

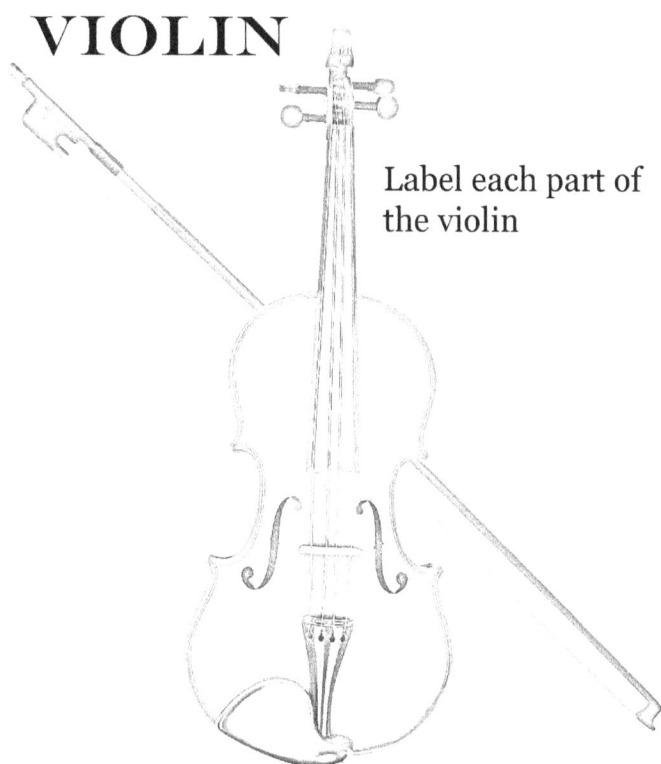

VIOLIN

Label each part of the violin

Genre：体裁, fusion：融合
Sub-genre：次类型，亚体裁
Instrument：乐器, stringed：有弦(乐器)的, wind：（管弦乐团的）管乐器，
percussion：打击乐器
Band：乐队, guitarist：吉他手, bassist：贝斯手, drummer：鼓手，
Keyboard player：键盘手
Vocalist, singer：歌手, backing vocals：伴唱, duet：二重奏（唱）
Rhythm：节奏
Lyrics：歌词
Producer：制作人
Miming：哑剧表演

20 Art

Focuses on painting and drawing.

Brainstorm Vocabulary

What do you know?

At the beginning of class, think of any vocabulary that you already know along with your classmates. If there is anything you don't know then <u>write it in the space below</u> and practice using it during class. Make sure you understand if it's a noun, verb, adjective or adverb. Make sure your pronunciation is accurate and that you know how to use it in a sentence. Is it formal or informal?

Write new vocabulary and expressions here:

Discussion

1: Why do we need art?

2: Public Art
Talk about some examples of public art that are in your city.
Do you think that money spent on public art is a waste?
There are surely many other more important things to spend our money on.

3: Famous works of art
Look at the pictures of famous works of art.
Listen and ask questions when your teacher talks about them.
What is your opinion about them? Do you like or dislike them? Why?
Make sure you practice some of the vocabulary from the beginning of class.

Tintoretto: Finding the Body of St Mark, 1548

Van Gogh: Self Portrait 1887-88

Van Gogh: Starry Night 1889

Georges Seurat: Sunday Afternoon on the Island of the Grande Jatte 1884

Pablo Picasso: Dora with Cat 1941

Andy Warhol: Marilyn Monroe 1962

Piet Mondrian: Composition with Red, Yellow and Blue 1921

Piet Mondrian: Composition with Red, Blue and Yellow 1921

Devil's Advocate

Photography is not Art.

Art should be taught in middle and high schools.

Role Play

Shopping for Art

Work in groups of three or four. Choose one work of art from below and sell it to your classmates.

Person A, B & C: You are a rich family. You want to buy some art for your new apartment in Shanghai as you are having a party soon. Visit an art gallery and see if they have anything you want to buy. Continually ask questions about this artwork.

Person D: Gallery owner. Sell some art to the family. Tell them about it and why it would look great in their apartment.

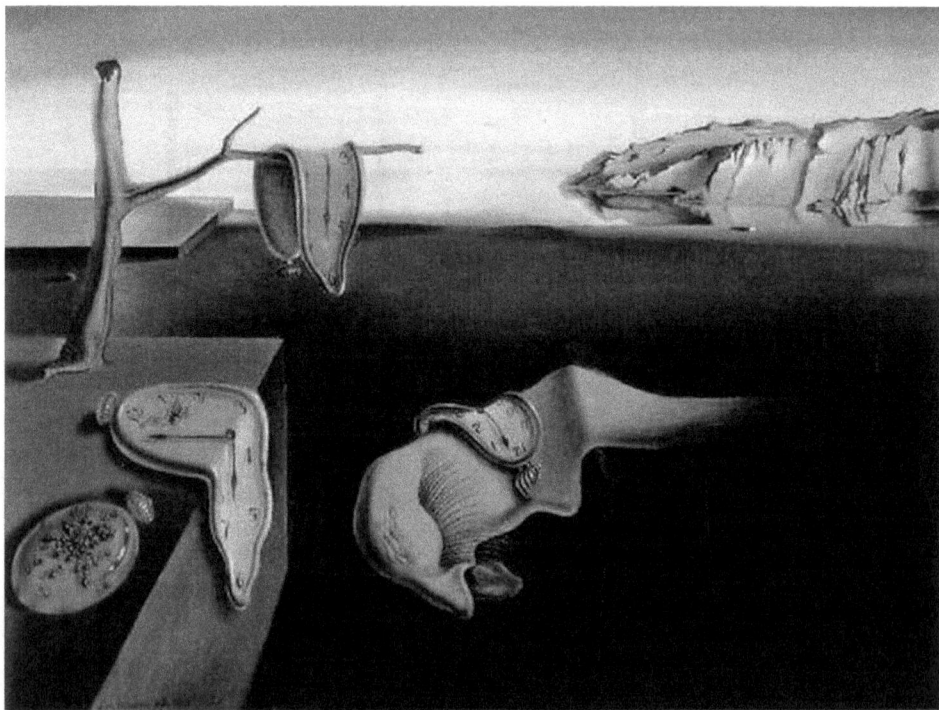

Salvador Dali: The Persistence of Memory 1931

Rodin: The Kiss 1889

Claude Monet: San Giorgio Maggiore at Dusk 1908

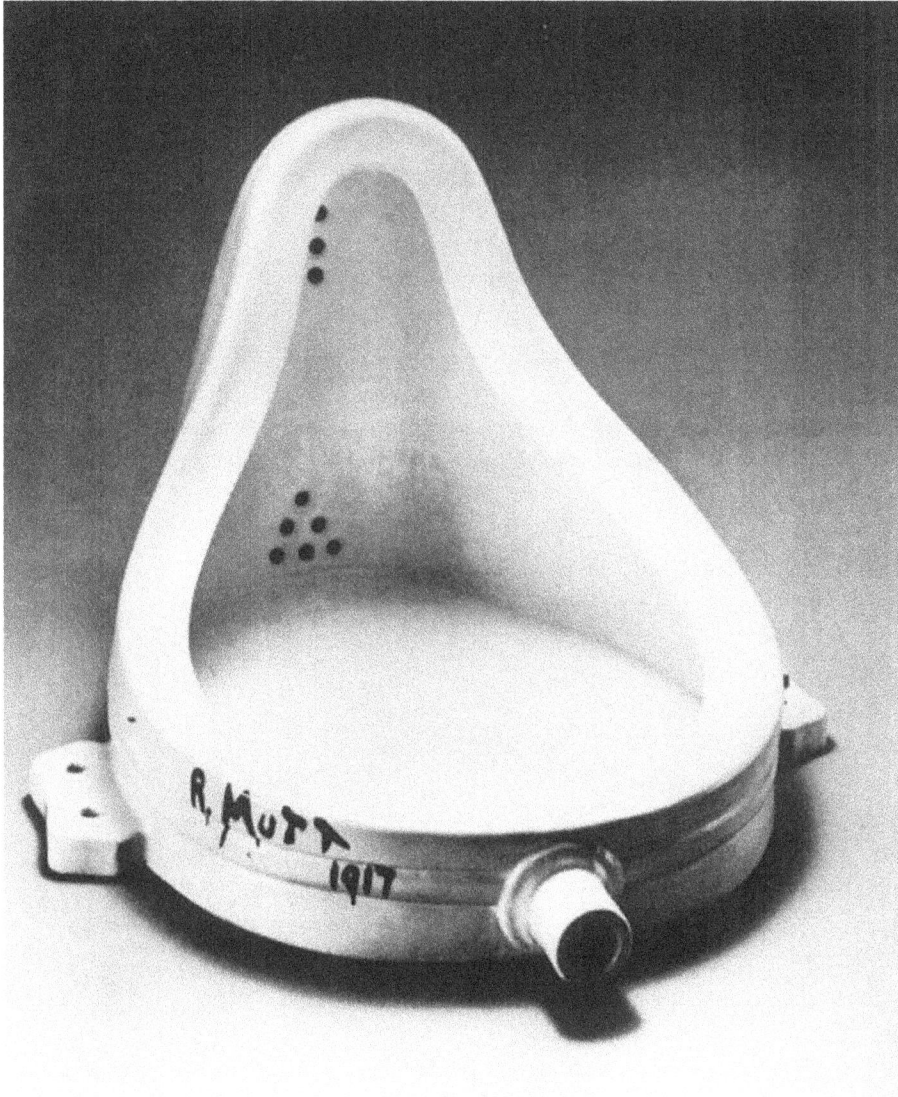

Marcel Duchamp: Fountain 1917

This is actually a toilet. It was thrown out of its first exhibition though was later voted the most important art of the twentieth century.

Finish Class

Additional Questions and Activities

1: BTQ: Talk about the last time you went to an art gallery (past tense)
When did you go? Which gallery?
Was there any art you really liked? Why did you like it?
Was there anything you disliked? Why?
If you have never been to an art gallery, why not?

2: What is Art?
If you see it in an art gallery does that make it art? Can anything be a work of art?

3: If you were an artist what kind of art would you be interested in?
Would it be painting, sculpture or <u>multi-media</u>? What genre and subject matter would interest you? Why?

4: Did you like Art at school? Why or why not? (past tense)
What was the best drawing or painting you ever did?

5: Is graffiti art? Why or why not?

<u>Roleplay</u>

Interview
<u>Person A:</u> Head Teacher.
Your school needs a new art teacher.
Interview this person for the job.
Ask interview questions, for example, about their experience etc.
<u>Person B:</u> Teacher.
How will you make your lessons interesting? Talk about your teaching methods.
Talk about your high standards of student achievement.

Visit a gallery
<u>Person A:</u> Artist.
Visit a popular gallery in Shanghai and ask if you can <u>exhibit</u> some of your work there.
<u>Person B:</u> Gallery owner.
You haven't heard of this artist before. Ask them about their art. What is their art about? Is it sculpture or painting?

College
Work in pairs or groups of three:
<u>Person A:</u> You are at college. You want to change your degree/major and study art. Tell your parents.
<u>Person B & C:</u> Parents. No way! They will never be able to support the family if they choose a life as an artist.

Vocabulary and useful expressions

Painting：油画, painter：画家

Materials: oil paints, water colour, pencils, ink：材料：油彩，水彩，铅笔，墨水

Canvas：油画布, water colour paper：水彩纸, brush：画笔

Primary and secondary colours：主要的和次要的颜色

2-dimensional, 2-D：二维, flat：平面

Illusion：幻想

Tone：色调, perspective：透视图, depth：深度, repetition：副本,

Implied movement：隐含的运动

Horizontal：水平线, vertical：垂直线, diagonal：对角线

Sculpture：雕刻, sculptor：雕刻家

Materials: stone, marble, granite, metal, clay, bronze：

材料：石头，大理石，花岗岩，金属，粘土，青铜

3-dimensional, 3-D：三维

Multi-media：多媒体, performance art：表演艺术, public art：公共艺术

Genre：类型

Subject Matter: landscape, cityscape, figure, portrait, abstract, still-life：

主题：景观，城市景观，人物，肖像，抽象，静物

History Timeline

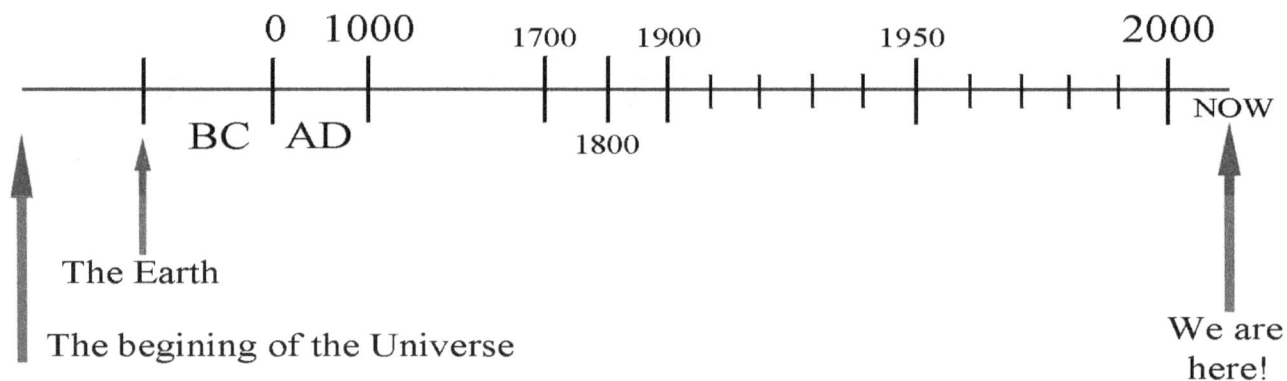

As you go through the lesson add vocabulary to the timeline or above and practice using it during class. Make sure you understand if it is a noun, verb, adjective or adverb etc. Make sure your pronunciation is accurate. Make sure you know how to use it in a sentence.
Is it formal or informal?

Discussion

1: What is the Big Bang Theory?
Work in groups of three.
If you don't know much about this, then think about it and guess.
Listen to your classmates. Your teacher will also work with you after.

2: What happened to the dinosaurs?
There are a few theories about this. What do you think?

3: BTQ: Talk about an important event in Chinese history (past tense)
What date was it?
What happened?
Why was it important?

4: BTQ: Talk about an important event in World history (past tense)
What date was it?
What happened?
Why was it important?

5: BTQ: Talk about a famous woman in history (past tense)
Why was she important?
What were her dates?
If you have time think of a famous Western woman in history.

6: Think of ten things you would see in a museum
Work individually and write your answers down.
The first student to reach ten should put their hand up and call out.

7: If you could go back in time
If you could go back in time and change one thing in history what would it be and why?

Devil's Advocate

We should learn about the history of our neighbouring countries such as Japan and Korea when we are at school.

Role Play

Visiting a Museum
Use the vocabulary from Question 6.
You can also <u>improvise</u> using any object at hand as a prop.
Work in small groups of three.

<u>Person A:</u> You are a tour group leader in a museum.
Welcome your visitors and introduce them to some of the many interesting exhibits.
Talk about their history and importance.
<u>Person B & C:</u> Visitors.
You are excited to be in the museum as it is your hobby.
However, you don't agree with some of the things the tour leader tells you.
Continually correct them and ask follow up questions.

Finish Class

Additional Questions and Activities

1: British Museum (past tense)
The British Museum has many Chinese relics.
What is their history? Why are they in a British museum and not a Chinese one?

2: Teacher Talk Time
The teacher can tell you something interesting about their country's history. Remember to listen and ask them questions so you can practice your English speaking.

3: Talk about the greatest inventions in history
What date were they made? Why are they important? Who invented them?
If you have any spare time, talk about the worst/most terrible inventions in history.

4: How old were you on New Year's Eve 1999?
Where were you and what can you remember about it?

5: 2008
2008 was known as 'China's Year'.
What happened to you during the Spring Festival that year? Did you travel by train? Tell your story. How about the rest of your family?

6: BTQ: Describe the last time you visited a museum (past tense)

Where did you go and when?

Did you enjoy it?

Who did you go with?

Which were the most interesting exhibits?

7: Ancestors (past tense)

Talk about the oldest relative that you know about in your family.

Where did they live? What did they do? Do you know any interesting stories about them?

Vocabulary and useful expressions

The Big Bang Theory：大爆炸理论

Genesis：起源

Prehistoric：史前的, dinosaurs：恐龙, asteroid：小行星, super-volcano：超级火山

BC (Before Christ): 公元前,

AD (Before Christ and Anno Domini meaning 'In the year of our Lord'): 公元

Ancient：远古的, civilizations：文明

Decade：十年, Century：世纪, Millennium：一千年

Early：早期的, mid：中间的, late twentieth century：二十世纪末期

The 60's, the 70's the 80's：60 年代，70 年代，80 年代

Archaeology：考古学, relics：遗迹, artifacts：史前古器物

22 Science

Mainly focuses on chemistry and physics.

Brainstorm Vocabulary

What do you know?

At the beginning of class, think of any vocabulary that you already know along with your classmates. If there is anything you don't know then <u>write it in the space below</u> and practice using it during class. Make sure you understand if it's a noun, verb, adjective or adverb. Make sure your pronunciation is accurate and that you know how to use it in a sentence. Is it formal or informal?

Write new vocabulary and expressions here:

Discussion

1: Which was your favourite science at school and why?
Also talk about your least favourite.

2: Talk about the greatest inventions in history (past tense)
What date were they made? Why are they important? Who invented them?

3: Talk about the worst/most terrible inventions in history (past tense)

4: Describe our lives in 100 years' time (future tense)
Talk about these aspects:
What will our homes be like, transport, leisure and in the office?

5: How are rainbows formed?

6: Cloning
Do you agree with cloning? Is it a good thing or a bad thing?
Would you like to have your own clone in case you got sick and needed to replace an organ? Maybe we can live forever if we keep replacing parts of our body?

Devil's Advocate

Machines do a better job than humans in factories.
We should invest in new technology to make our industry more efficient.

Role Play

An Ancient Chinese Invention
Person A: You live in ancient China. You have invented paper. Sell your new idea to a local business person.
Person B: Local business person. This idea is crazy! Why should you buy this strange new thing called 'paper'?

Science Teacher
You can use the interview questions found in T14.

<u>Person A:</u> You are the head teacher of a middle school.
You need to hire a science teacher. Interview a specialist for the job. Ask interview questions such as how long have you been interested in science?
<u>Person B:</u> Teacher.
What is your experience?
Have you always been a teacher? What did you do before?
What ideas do you have to make interesting lessons?

Finish Class

Additional Questions and Activities

1: What will our computers be like in the future? (future tense)
You can replace this with almost anything from any topic such as transport, homes, TV, mobile phones and shopping; you name it!

2: A.I.
In the future our machines may be able to think for themselves. Do you think having 'smart' technology is a good thing?

3: Modifying Genes
Is changing something's genes a good or bad thing?
In what ways will we be able to alter something's genes in the future?
What dangers are there if you alter something's genes?

4: Deep space travel
Do you think we will ever travel to other planets? What do you think our space craft would like? How would humans be able to travel such long distances?

5: Thunder & Lightning
How can you <u>tell</u> how far away a thunder storm is?
What precautions could you take if you were in a storm in the countryside away from any shelter? What should you not do and why?

6: How does modern technology make our lives more convenient?
When can it be inconvenient for our lives?

7: How do you make fire?

Vocabulary and useful expressions

Chemistry：化学, physics：物理, biology：生物学

Periodic table：（元素）周期表, elements：要素

Atom：原子, electron：电子, proton (outside)：质子, neutron (inside an atom)：中子

Quark (forms neutrons and protons): 夸克, molecule：分子

States：状态, gas：气体, solid：固体, liquid：液体

Freeze：凝固, melt：融化, vaporize：蒸发, condense：凝结

Experiment：实验

Friction：摩擦, refraction：折射, gravity：重力，万有引力

Conductor：导体, insulator：绝缘体

Topic
23 The Supernatural

Brainstorm Vocabulary

What do you know?

At the beginning of class, think of any vocabulary that you already know along with your classmates. If there is anything you don't know then <u>write it in the space below</u> and practice using it during class. Make sure you understand if it's a noun, verb, adjective or adverb. Make sure your pronunciation is accurate and that you know how to use it in a sentence. Is it formal or informal?

Write new vocabulary and expressions here:

Discussion

1: Talk about something strange you have experienced (past tense)
It may also be something a family member or friend experienced.
It could be something that you saw on TV, on the internet or read about somewhere.

2: UFO's
Do you believe that there is life on other planets? Why or why not?
Do you believe that we have been visited by aliens? Why of why not?

3: Crop Circles
In pairs, look at the handout to look at the photograph of a crop circle at the end of the topic. Read the information at the bottom of the photo.
Do you think the circle in the photo is real or a fake? Why?
What do you think creates a crop circle? Is it all just a <u>hoax</u>?

4: Superstitions
Are you superstitious? Why or why not?
What are some popular superstitions in China?
Which numbers are lucky and unlucky? Why?
Do you have any lucky objects? Do you carry them with you?

5: Fear
Think of two things that you are afraid of. Why are you afraid of them?

6: What happens after you die?
In this question we are talking about your spirit or soul. The discussion is not just the physical side of being cremated/burnt or buried.
If you think there is nothing after death why do you believe this?
If you think there is something more than just death, what is it? Why do you have this belief?

7: Would you like to attend a <u>séance</u>? Why or why not?
If you were invited, would you use a <u>ouija board</u> and try and communicate with spirits? Why or why not?

8: Tell a ghost story
It could be something that happened to you, friends or family. It could be something you read about or saw on TV.

Finish Class

Crop Circles

Fact or Fake?

Crop Circle: Wiltshire 2001

This one had 409 circles and was 900 feet in diameter.
It was made on a curved hill so you could not see from one side to the other.

It appeared one Saturday night while it was raining. A plane flew over the hill the day before and there was nothing there. It was found on Sunday morning.

Could this be a hoax? Think about it:
There are 409 circles
If a team of 12 people in pairs did it, that would be 68 circles for each pair.
If you allowed each pair 10 minutes to make each circle that would therefore be 680 minutes.
That's 11 hours with no break at night and in the rain.
If you doubled the number of people that would still be 24 people working for 5 hours with no break.

What do you think?

142

Vocabulary and useful expressions

Skeptic：怀疑论者, hoax：恶作剧

Mysterious：神秘的, strange：奇怪的, weird：怪异的, unexplained：无法解释的

UFO：不明飞行物, ET's, aliens：外星人, abducted：劫持

Crop circle：麦田里的怪圈

Superstition：迷信

Fate, destiny：命运

Premonition：预兆, clairvoyance：洞察力

Reincarnation：再生, spirit：精神, soul：灵魂, karma：<宗>因果报应

Out of body experience：灵魂出窍

Haunted：闹鬼的, apparition：幽灵,

Séance (meeting to contact ghost), 与鬼魂接触的会以

Ouija board /wɪdʒə/ or / wɪdʒi/：灵应牌

Poltergeist：敲击作响闹恶作剧的鬼

Appendix A

Grammar at a Glance

Article:
Definite Article: *the* is used to restrict the meaning of a noun and give us information about it **Indefinite Article:** a determiner that expresses non-specific reference, such as *a, an,* or *some*

Preposition:
used before <u>nouns</u>, pronouns, or other substantives to form <u>phrases</u> functioning as modifiers of <u>verbs</u>, nouns, or <u>adjectives</u>, and that typically express a spatial, temporal, or other relationship, **as in, on, by, to, since, at, of, off, with.**

A <u>part of speech</u> that indicates the relationship, often spatial, of one word to another, for example, 'She paused <u>at</u> the door', 'This apple is ripe <u>for</u> picking'; and 'They talked the matter over face <u>to</u> face.' Some common prepositions are ***at, by, for, from, in, into, on, to, and with.***

Noun:
Nouns are a class of words that are subjects of verbs and prepositions. They can be used in plurals. Nouns often refer to people, places, things, states and quantities.

Subject Pronoun:
What are <u>you</u> looking at? e.g. **I, me, you, him, he, she, this, who, what** takes the place of a noun.

Verb:
Verbs are used to describe actions, states and relationships between two or more things.

Adjective:
Adjectives describe and modify nouns or pronouns. They can be before such as the red car or after such as the car is red.

Adverb: Adverbs are used to modify a **verb, an adjective, or another adverb**:

1: Mary sings *terribly*
2: David is *extremely* stupid
3: This car goes *incredibly* slow

In 1, the adverb *beautifully* tells us how Mary sings. In 2, *extremely* tells us the degree to which David is stupid. Finally, in 3, the adverb *incredibly* tells us how slowly the car goes.

Many adverbs end in ly e.g. slowly, quickly, softly, suddenly, and gradually
Adjectives: slow, quick, soft, sudden, gradual

Adverbs are gradable e.g. soft = very softly, extremely quickly, really gently
These modifying words are also adverbs and called **Degree Adverbs**
(almost, barely, entirely, highly, quite, slightly, totally, and utterly)

Comparative Adverbs: use more e.g. more recently, more frequently
Superlative Adverbs: use most e.g. most recently, most frequently

Adverbs do not modify nouns.

Phrasal Verbs: When a verb is added to a preposition or adverb the meaning of the verb changes, for example, 'My car broke down last night' > break down. Phrasal verbs can have more than one meaning. In this case someone who is upset can break down.

There are around 3,000 phrasal verbs. They are impossible to quantify due to informal and formal usage.

Some are <u>**separable**</u> and can be split up and still form a sentence:
'Take off your coat' > 'Take your coat off.'
'She looked up the word' > 'She looked the word up'
'He ate up all his dinner' >'He ate all his dinner up'.

Some are <u>**inseparable**</u>
'We are looking into the problem.' (would be *looking the problem into*)
'Look after the children.' (would be *look the children after*)
'I called on a friend' (would be I called a friend on)

Predicate: Every complete sentence contains two parts: a **subject** and a **predicate**. The subject is what (or whom) the sentence is about, while the predicate tells something about the subject. In the following sentences, the predicate is placed in brackets ( ), while the subject is highlighted.

Barry (runs).
Barry and his dog (run on the hill every morning).

Coordinating Conjunction: join or link words or phrases together within a sentence. Some coordinating conjunctions are **and, yet, for, and but.**

Subordinating Conjunctions: are found at the beginning of independent clauses. Some common subordinating conjunctions are **if, although, since and while.**

Demonstrative Determiner: used to <u>demonstrate</u> the <u>identity</u> of the thing referenced by the following <u>noun</u>; in <u>English</u>, they include **<u>this</u>, <u>these</u>, <u>that</u> and <u>those</u>** e.g. 'I like this dictionary' the word 'this' is a demonstrative determiner.

Clause: is a group of words which act as a single unit and is built round a verb, for example, 'he lives in the UK'

Compound and complex sentences contain two or more clauses:

Simple: **'Barry is living in the UK'.**

Compound: **'<u>He lives in the UK</u>,** but <u>his family is still in China'</u>.

Complex: 'While his family is still in China, <u>Barry is staying with friends'</u>.

Relative Clauses: A sentence or statement that can give extra information. They can bring two parts of a sentence together to make dialogue more <u>fluent</u>. To do this we use **relative pronouns,** for example, 'A girl is talking to Tom. Do you know the girl?'>'Do you know the girl <u>who</u> is talking to Tom?'

- **That:** Subject or Object pronoun for people, animals or things
- **Who:** Subject or Object for people
- **Which:** Subject or Object for animals or things
- **Which:** Referring to a whole sentence, for example, 'He couldn't say the letter T which surprised me'.
- **Whose:** Possession for animals or things

If Clauses: There are three types of conditional if-clauses
- Conditional Sentence 1: Here it is possible and also very probable that the condition will be completed:
Form: If + simple present = will (future)
E.g.: If I see his wife, Ill tell her he's down the bar.
- Conditional Sentence 2: Here it is possible but unlikely, that the condition will be completed.
Form: If + simple past = conditional (would + infinitive)
E.g.: If I saw his wife, I would tell her he was down the bar.

- Conditional Sentence 3: Here it is impossible that the condition will be completed because it is referring to the past.

Form: If + past perfect = conditional (would have + past participle)

Example: If I had seen his wife, I would have told her he was down the bar.

3rd Person – Simple present tense: he, she, them and they

'Joe walks down the street with his hands in his pockets'.

'She stares into the mirror at the failure before her'.

- **He/She**: Third person singular
- **It:** Third person singular
- **They**: Third person plural

2nd Person – Simple present tense: You stare into the mirror at the failure before you.

- **You**: Second person singular

1st Person – Simple present tense: I stare into the mirror at the failure before me 1st

- **I**: First person singular
- **We**: First person plural

VERB FORMS

Lexical Verb: contain some sort of meaning and can stand alone, e.g. 'I love chocolate'

Auxiliary Verb: 1: help the lexical verb e.g. 'He's watching TV' = 'is'

      2: to make the sentence 'He lives here' negative, add does to make 'He doesn't live here'

      3: to create a question 'Does he live here?'

Remember: **be, do and have** can function in different forms.

Remember: be has different present and past forms: am, are is, has and were

However, all three can be used as lexical and auxiliary verbs as well e.g.

'I didn't arrive on time' + auxiliary

'I did my homework' = lexical only

Modal Auxiliary Verbs: carry meaning: can, could, may, might, will, would, shall, should, must, need, ought to and dare e.g. 'I must go'.

Base Form of a verb: e.g. 'He listens' the base form is to listen.

Present Participle ends in 'ing'. Are verb forms used to function as an adjective. They are the only verb forms that stay completely regular (see below).

The present participle is used with an auxiliary to express the progressive aspect (see below)
'That film is very exciting'

Past Participle ends in 'ed' or 'en' and it has two functions:

1) Adjective

E.g.: This car **is** <u>heated</u>. (Verb: 'is'; Adjective 'heated')
E.g.: We had **a** <u>heated</u> discussion. (Adjective 'heated')
E.g.: I had seen it, I have seen it, I will have seen it, It was seen

As an adjective, the past participle occurs after the verb **BE** (is, am, was, were, been) or it modifies a noun.

2) As part of a verb

E.g.: The stove **has** <u>heated</u> the room. (Verb: 'has'; Part of a verb: 'heated')

As a part of a verb, the past participle occurs with the verb **HAVE** (have, has, had).

Gerunds: verb + ing 'I'm working as hard as I can' or 'Running is good for your health'
They are only formed with the infinitive + ing
Note the difference between a progressive which uses is was has have would etc
Gerund: A verb form with 'ing' forming a noun, for example, 'I am going <u>running</u>'.

S-Forms: she plays, he works

Ing-Forms: playing, running

Finite Verbs: form the main part of a sentence. Non-finite is therefore an infinitive, gerund or participle

Infinitives: Verbs that have to before them. Sometimes they will be no to but the verb still remains the infinitive such as feel, hear, help, make, let, see and watch.

Action Verbs/State Verbs: 'Nigel went to school' = action. 'I'm buying a new car' = action
                          'Nigel was busy' = state. 'I need a new car' = state
'Action' is something happening e.g. do, go buy, play stop, take
'State' is something staying the same e.g. be, doubt, believe, know, want, need, seem

Regulars Verbs: Most verbs are regular. If we add 'ed' to them to put them into the past, the spelling or pronunciation is the same. 'I walked' can be used in past tense or past participle,
'I walked', 'I have walked'

Irregular Verbs: (around 400) Their sound or spelling changes when we put them into the past, for example, 'make = made', 'give = gave(s) or given (pp)', 'saw = seen'
Was, bite, bring, break, bought, and began
Some irregular verbs are the same in past simple and past participle e.g. make/made/made

Mixing different verb forms to create phrases:
1. e.g. Combine irregular v 'have' as an auxiliary to the – **ing** lexical 'be'
'I have been'
2. e.g. Combine modal 'should' with base form 'have' and past participle of 'study'
'I should have studied'

Past Tense refers to a verb, (remember that past participles are not verbs.)

E.g.: The stove <u>heated</u> the room.
E.g.: I saw it

In the example above, the word heated doesnt do the following things:

It doesn't occur with BE (is, am, was, were, been)
It doesn't occur with HAVE (have, has, have)
It doesnt modify a noun (argument)

'heated' functions all by itself. It's a verb, and the 'ed' ending tells us it's a past tense verb

Present Perfect: **Actually still refers to a past event:** We use the Present Perfect to say that an action happened at an unspecified time before now. The exact time is not important. You CANNOT use the Present Perfect with specific time expressions such as: yesterday, one year ago, last week, when I was a child, when I lived in China, at that moment, that day, one day, etc. We CAN use the Present Perfect with unspecific expressions such as: ever, never, once, many times, several times, before, so far, already, yet, etc.
Present Perfect examples:
I **have seen** that film twenty times.
I think I **have met** him once before.
There **have been** many earthquakes in Japan.
People **have travelled** to the Moon.
People **have not travelled** to Jupiter.
Have you **read** the book yet?
Nobody **has** ever **climbed** that mountain.

A: **Has** there ever **been** a war in Europe?
B: Yes, there **has been** a war in the Europe.

Past Perfect: The Past Perfect expresses the idea that something occurred before another action in the past. It can also show that something happened before a specific time in the past.
I **had** never **seen** such a beautiful beach before I went to Kauai.
I did not have any money because I **had lost** my wallet.
Tony knew Istanbul so well because he **had visited** the city several times.

Future perfect: The Future Perfect expresses the idea that something will occur before another action in the future. It can also show that something will happen before a specific time in the future.
By next November, I **will have received** my promotion.
By the time he *gets* home, she **is going to have cleaned** the entire house.
I **am not going to have finished** this test by 3 o'clock.

Progressive Aspect: also called Continuous uses 'to be'

A. Present progressive = am + (base form + -ing): I am working OR is + (base form + -ing):
She is eating. OR are + (base form + -ing): We are studying.

1. A planned activity: Sofia is starting school at CEC tomorrow

2. An activity that is occurring right now: Jan is watching TV right now.

3. An activity that is in progress, although not actually occurring at the time of speaking: Sara is learning English at CEC.

B. Past progressive = was + (base form + -ing): I was working. OR were + (base form + -ing): They were eating.

1. A past activity in progress while another activity occurred: At 6:00 yesterday I was eating dinner. The phone rang while I was eating.

2. Two past activities in progress at the same time: While I was answering the phone, my wife was cooking dinner.

C. Future progressive = will be + (base form + -ing): I will be working. He will be eating.

An activity that will be in progress: This time next year we will be living in Canada.

We can also ask about someone's plans using the future progressive.
Will you be going to Canada next year?

D. Present perfect progressive = have + (base form + -ing): I have been working. OR has + (base form + -ing): She has been eating.

 1. This tense emphasizes the duration of an activity that began in the past and continues into the present. It often uses time words or phrases. It may be used to refer to continuing activity that is recent: He has been painting houses all summer. I've been studying English for 2 years.

2. It may be used to refer to continuing activity that is recent: He has been going to school at CEC.

E. Past perfect progressive = had + (base form + -ing): I had been working. He had been eating.

When the teacher arrived, I had been waiting almost 10 minutes. He was out of breath because he had been running to catch the bus.

F. Future perfect progressive = will have + (base form + -ing): I will have been working. She will have been eating. This tense emphasizes the duration of a continuing activity in the future that ends before another activity or time in the future.

By 2003 Janet will have been studying English at CEC for 3 years. By 9:45 tonight I will have been sitting in class for 2 hours and 45 minutes.

Active Verbs (voice): In active sentences, the thing doing the action is the subject of the sentence and the thing receiving the action is the object. <u>Most sentences we say are active</u>.

(Thing doing action) + (verb) + (thing receiving action)

The teacher (subject) teaches (active verb) the students (object)
Students (subject) do (active verb) their homework (object)

Passive Verbs (voice): In passive sentences, the thing <u>receiving</u> the action is the subject of the sentence and the thing doing the action is optionally included near the end of the sentence.

(Thing receiving action) + (be) + (past participle of verb) + (by) + (thing doing action)

The students (sub) are taught (passive verb) by the teacher (object)
Homework (sub) is done (passive verb) by the students (object)

Using Phonetics

A basic knowledge of phonetics is very useful and most Chinese students use it as a guide in their pronunciation. Write the relevant symbol under new vocabulary if you are having problems with pronunciation. The various symbols plus examples are below. The sounds where students have the most frequent difficulties are interlined.

Iː	I	ʊ	uː	Iə	eI	
fleece	minute	foot	group	near	face	
e	ə	ɜː	ɔː	ʊə	ɔI	əʊ
head	common	nurse	thought	store	choice	show
æ	ʌ	ɑː	ɒ	eə	ɑI	ɑʊ
track	love	start	lot	fair	high	round
p	b	t	d	ʧ	ʤ	k	g
plant	black	trust	ladder	church	judge	key	get
f	v	θ	ð	s	z	ʃ	ʒ
future	heavy	thank	this	soon	zoo	ship	usual
m	n	ŋ	h	l	r	w	j
mountain	Nigeria	king	heavy	valley	robin	windy	useful

Consonants

p: pen, copy, happen
b: back, baby, job
t: tea, tight, button
d: day, ladder, odd
k: key, clock, school
g: get, giggle, ghost
tʃ: church, match, nature
dʒ: judge, age, soldier
f: fat, coffee, rough, photo
v: view, heavy, move
θ: thing, author, path
ð: this, other, smooth
s: soon, cease, sister
z: zero, music, roses, buzz
ʃ: ship, sure, national
ʒ: pleasure, vision
h: hot, whole, ahead
m: more, hammer, sum
n: nice, know, funny, sun
ŋ: ring, anger, thanks, sung
l: light, valley, feel
r: right, wrong, sorry, arrange
j: use, beauty, few
w: wet, one, when, queen
ʔ: (glottal stop)department, football
(often used in the UK)

Vowels

ɪ: kit, bid, hymn, minute
e: dress, bed, head, many
æ: trap, bad
ɒ: lot, odd, wash
ʌ: strut, mud, love, blood
ʊ: foot, good, put
iː: fleece, sea, machine
eɪ: face, day, break
aɪ: price, high, try
ɔɪ: choice, boy
uː: goose, two, blue, group
əʊ: goat, show, no
aʊ: mouth, now, brown
ɪə: near, here, weary
eə: square. fair, various
ɑː: start, father
ɔː: thought, law, north, war
ʊə: poor, jury, cure
ɜː nurse, stir, learn, refer
ə: about, common, standard
i: happy, radiate. glorious
u: thank you, influence, situation

153

www.ingramcontent.com/pod-product-compliance
Lightning Source LLC
Chambersburg PA
CBHW081212020426
42331CB00012B/3001